ESSENTIALS
of Credit, Collections, and Accounts Receivable

D0877763

Essentials Series

The Essentials Series was created for busy business advisory and corporate professionals. The books in this series were designed so that these busy professionals can quickly acquire knowledge and skills in core business areas.

Each book provides need-to-have fundamentals for those professionals who must:

- Get up to speed quickly, because they have been promoted to a new position or have broadened their responsibility scope

- Manage a new functional area

- Brush up on new developments in their area of responsibility

- Add more value to their company or clients

Other books in this series include:

Essentials of Accounts Payable, by Mary S. Schaeffer

Essentials of Capacity Management, by Reginald Tomas Yu-Lee

Essentials of CRM: A Guide to Customer Relationship Management, by Bryan Bergeron

Essentials of Intellectual Property, by Alexander I. Poltorak and Paul J. Lerner

Essentials of Trademarks and Unfair Competition, by Dana Shilling

Essentials of Corporate Performance Measurement, by George T. Friedlob, Lydia L.F. Schleifer and Franklin J. Plewa, Jr.

For more information on any of the above titles, please visit www.wiley.com.

ESSENTIALS

of Credit, Collections, and Accounts Receivable

Mary S. Schaeffer

WILEY

Library of Congress Cataloging-in-Publication Data

Schaeffer, Mary S.
  Essentials of credit, collections, and accounts receivable / Mary S. Schaeffer.
    p. cm.
  ISBN 0-471-22074-4 (pbk : alk. paper)
  1. Credit—Management. I. Title.
  HG3751 .S334 2002
  658.8'8—dc21   2002005070

Printed in the United States of America.

10 9 8 7 6 5 4 3

For my princess,
Larissa Mary Noelle Ludwig,
my wonderful, beautiful, gifted daughter

Contents

1 The First Step: Approving the Credit   1

2 The Second Step: Billing   29

3 The Third Step: Collecting the Money   49

4 Accounts Receivable Issues   81

5 Handling Deduction Issues   103

6 Interacting with Sales and Marketing   115

7 Customer Relations and Customer Visits   133

8 Letters of Credit and Other Security Interests   147

9 Legal Considerations Surrounding Credit   163

10 Bankruptcy   183

11 Technology in the Credit and Collections Department   215

12 Professionalism and the Future of the Credit Profession   241

Index   253

Preface

redit is part science, part art, and part gut-feel. The trick is to get the right mix. While there is no one absolute right way to handle the credit, collections, and accounts receivable functions, there are a few that are totally and irrefutably wrong. It is the mission of this book to identify both for the reader.

For the last eight plus years, I have been lucky enough to spend my days talking to credit professionals and writing about their successes and achievements, their trials and tribulations, and occasionally their catastrophes as a newsletter editor for *IOMA's Report on Managing Credit Receivables and Collections.* Much of what they have told me is reflected in this book. Thus, the suggestions and recommendations are not pie-in-the-sky advice but rather practical guidance based on real life accomplishments and failures.

Before reviewing what is covered in the book, I'd like to point out that there are many ways these functions can be handled. Often what works at one company will not at the next. This can be because the second company doesn't have the technology of the first, and because the corporate culture is very different or can be simply due to differing industry requirements. Thus, many of the topics in the Tips & Techniques will cover a variety of approaches—some applicable to more sophisticated companies and some to the less advanced.

The book starts with a look at approving credit. This should be the first step for companies before they begin a relationship with a new customer —although as many reading this are only too well aware, it occasionally occurs after the fact, after the salesperson has taken the order. Chapter 1 begins with an explanation of why business credit is so important, verifies that a business does exist, and examines financial statements in detail. The chapter takes a look at the way companies evaluate credit, the information many require on their credit applications, and the references many require. Ratio analysis, how companies evaluate new customers, and what documentation should be in the credit file are also examined.

Many companies overlook the importance of their billing practices in the credit and collection process. An invoice mailed late will get a payment posted even later. Chapter 2 takes an in-depth look at invoices, the best way to design an invoice and best billing practices. An outsider might not realize that there are many things companies can and should do to their invoices to improve their ability to collect in the most timely and efficient manner and ultimately the company's bottom line.

Electronic invoicing is one of the hottest topics in the credit arena today. Chapter 2 takes a look at the practice and also offers details about five of the products on the market today. Electronic invoicing is likely to have a big impact on business in the next few years, and thus it is imperative that credit and collection professionals learn everything they can about it.

The book then goes on to take a look at the thankless task of collecting. Many in the collection profession feel that at best they break even. If they do a good job, no one notices, but the moment collections slip, management is watching them like a hawk and complaining. Unfortunately, many who have this complaint are quite accurate. Chapter 3 contains numerous tips that have worked for professionals in the field today. We look at both the old-fashioned letter writing and the more current practices of phoning, e-mailing, faxing, and whatever else innovative collection professionals can dream up to get the money in the bank for their companies.

Applying cash is another thankless job in corporate America today. However, if the task is not handled correctly it causes problems for other professionals in the company and, in some extreme cases, can tarnish the company's reputation with prized customers. Chapter 4 looks at some effective accounts receivable strategies along with a discussion of the vaunted days sales outstanding (DSO) figures that so many credit and collection professionals are measured against.

Unauthorized deductions, along with unearned discounts, cause credit professionals in certain industries (mainly those selling to retailers) more headaches than almost anything else. Chapter 5 examines strategies companies can use to minimize this haunting problem. The chapter also takes a look at techniques to use for timely dispute resolution as a few customers will use a small dispute (some say, imagined) to avoid paying large invoices.

A smooth relationship with sales and marketing can make a big difference in the amount of Tylenol a credit professional must buy each year. Some lucky credit professionals have wonderful dealings with their sales force. Chapter 6 discusses the strategies used to either maintain or initiate a warm relationship with sales. Also included are some things the credit department can do to make the sales force's job just a little bit easier. Yes, you read that right—if credit goes out of its way to help sales, it will reap the rewards.

Most credit professionals insist that customer visits are key to completely and accurately evaluating a customer's financial viability. Unfortunately, some management don't agree. This is unfortunate because when a customer gets into financial difficulty and has a limited amount of money to pay suppliers, after paying key suppliers, it is most likely to pay those it has the best relationship with—and inevitably, those are the ones where personal contact has been made with the credit professional. Chapter 7 looks at the best ways to plan and structure a customer visit along with some ways credit pros can squeeze in customer visits so even the stingiest of bosses can't complain.

Inevitably, the sales department will eventually (or perhaps immediately) find a potential customer who does not meet the company's credit standards for open account terms. When this happens, the savvy credit pro finds a way to make the sale happen—usually by getting some sort of security. Chapter 8 examines some of the techniques that credit professionals can recommend in order to make the sale happen.

Some professionals think that credit professionals really need to be lawyers first. There are a number of laws that credit professionals must know about and avoid breaking as part of their job. Chapter 9 takes a look at some of the legal considerations surrounding credit and collection activity.

Perhaps one of the most fascinating aspects of credit is bankruptcy. It is a regular part of most credit managers' jobs no matter how good they are. Chapter 10 describes the different types of bankruptcies, the rights of creditors, and what creditors should do to secure their positions. It also takes a look at what some consider one of the nastiest aspects of bankruptcy—preferences. A preferential situation arises when all creditors in the same class are not treated the same. If one or more has received a payment that the courts deem to be preferential, they are ordered to return it to the bankrupt company's estate. This chapter discusses some of the ways that a creditor hit with a preference claim can fight that claim.

Without a doubt, the credit profession has changed more in the last ten years than it did in the previous 20. Many of these changes can be attributed to technology and the things that credit professionals can do as a result of the introduction of many technological advances. Chapter 11 takes an in-depth look at technology currently in use in today's leading-edge credit departments.

The credit profession has undergone revolution. This roller coaster change is only at the first curve. The skill set required of the credit professional in the coming years continues to expand. Chapter 12 takes a look at a number of resources credit, collection, and accounts receivable professionals can use in the upcoming years to keep themselves in the credit game. Those who sit still will not succeed, but you've already taken the first step by purchasing this book.

Good luck—it will be an exciting adventure for those who choose to participate.

Acknowledgments

Throughout this book you will see mention of a company called IOMA (Institute of Management and Administration), a New York City-based newsletter publisher. IOMA is the company I work for and the publisher of, among many others, a monthly newsletter called *IOMA's Report on Managing Credit, Receivables & Collections.* In my position as editor of this publication since 1994, I have had the opportunity to interact with hundreds of credit and collections professionals and the vendors who provide services to the credit community. It is from these discussions that I am able to develop new material—not only for the newsletter each month, but also for this book.

Additional material for my publications comes from the original research conducted by IOMA in the form of an annual survey where credit professionals from around the country share information about what they are doing, what technology they are using, and how they are evaluating their current and potential customers. Also, material presented at credit-specific conferences is helpful in breaking new trends.

Without the backing of IOMA, this information would not be as readily available. In its ongoing commitment to provide the best information possible to the business community, IOMA also makes trial subscriptions to its newsletters available to those who request them either by calling its customer service department at (212) 244-0360 or through its Web site at www.ioma.com.

A special thanks must go to both Perry Patterson, the company's vice president and publisher, and David Foster, IOMA's president, for making all this happen.

CHAPTER 1

The First Step: Approving the Credit

After reading this chapter you will be able to

- Understand the importance of accurately evaluating credit
- Evaluate the creditworthiness of customers
- Understand the different types of financial statements
- Identify the warning signs of customers in trouble

There is an old adage in credit that says a sale is not a sale until the invoice is paid. Until that point, it is a gift. It is the primary responsibility of the credit department to make sure that the company converts all those gifts into sales. It is also the job of the credit department to make sure that sales are made to companies that have both the ability and the willingness to pay for the goods.

Why Business Credit Is Important

Finding the right credit policy is a mixture of art and science. Many issues affect the policy. Corporate culture, the company's margins, competition, existing inventory, and seasonality are just a few of the matters to be considered, in addition to the obvious financial analysis. When credit is extended to a company that cannot or will not pay, the impact directly impacts the seller's bottom line. More insidious, when the seller pays late, there is a bottom line impact as well, although it is not as apparent. Similarly, when a buyer takes unauthorized deductions the action impacts the bottom line—sometimes to the point of making the sale unprofitable. Let's look at a simple example. Here are the facts:

- Company A sells company B $1,000 worth of widgets.
- The company has a 5% margin.
- Company A is paying 6% interest on its bank loans.
- Payment is expected in 30 days.
- Company B pays the invoice 60 days late.
- Company B takes a deduction for $45 for a variety of minor issues.

There should be a $50 profit on the sale ($1,000 x .05). In a 6% interest rate environment, the 60-day late payment results in an extra payment to the bank of $10 ($1,000 x .06/12 x 60/360). In this case, however, there is a loss of $5 on the sale ($50 − $10 − $45). Yet, few within the company would realize there had been a loss and sales would continue in this pattern. Now, many reading this may be thinking that deductions of this magnitude do not occur; let me assure you that in many industries they do.

Now, let's assume that the company in the example above never paid. The $1,000 is written off as bad debt. To make up for the bad debt, the company would have to sell $19,000 (($1,000 − $50)/.05) just to break even on the invoice that was not paid.

If the credit staff does its job correctly, neither loss will occur. Later in this chapter, we will discuss those occasions when credit standards may be loosened to intentionally allow for bad debt. This is sometimes done when a company decides that the bad debt written off will be more than compensated for by additional sales.

Sales Prevention Department—Not!

As can be seen from the simple examples above, the functions of the credit department often come in direct conflict with the sales department. This sometimes leads the sales department to refer to the credit department as the sales prevention department. Nothing could be further from the truth. It is the function of the credit department to work to make sales (not gifts) happen—if at all feasible. Chapter 6 will introduce you to a variety of ways that sales and credit can work together.

Open Account

Credit would not be a problem if companies bought and sold goods the way individuals do. When most people need something, they go to the store and either pay cash or use a credit card. In either case, the store gets its money within a day or two. Businesses do not operate in that manner. The preferred way of operating (at least from the seller's standpoint) is to order goods and pay for them at a later date. This is referred to as *open account*. When goods are sold on open account terms, the seller ships the merchandise and then expects to be paid at some point in the future, say 30 days after the buyer receives the goods.

Discounts for Early Payment

In many industries, a discount is offered for early payment. The most common discount offered is 2% discount if the invoice is paid within ten days. You may remember seeing the term 2/10 net 30 in your old accounting books. If it is not paid within the discount period, then the full amount is due on the due date, which in the example here would be 30 days. Other terms sometimes seen include 1/7 net 10 or 2/10 net 11. The first allows the buyer to take a 1% discount if the invoice is paid in seven days, otherwise the total is due in ten days. The latter permits a 2% discount if the invoice is paid within the first ten days, otherwise the total is due in 11 days. In both of these examples, it is expected that the purchaser will take the discount unless it is experiencing financial problems.

Those who have been in the profession for some time are probably aware that many buyers take the discount and do not pay within the discount period. This is referred to as an *unearned discount*. In some industries this is a massive problem. Techniques to deal with this issue will be discussed in great detail in Chapter 5.

Terms Preferred by Sellers

Most sellers would like to sell on a cash-in-advance (CIA) basis. The problem with CIA terms is that, with very minor exceptions, few companies would purchase under those conditions. Thus, companies, and more specifically the credit staff, need to find ways to quantify risk and identify those customers who will pay if sold on open account terms. They also need to find ways to sell to those who don't "qualify" for open account terms. These alternatives are discussed in Chapter 8.

Credit Reports

Most credit professionals begin building their "credit case" with a credit report, usually pulled from Dun & Bradstreet (D&B), although specialty reports are available from other agencies. Even if only a minimal credit investigation is to be done because the potential sale is small, many credit professionals still pull a credit report to verify that the business is legitimate and not a fly-by-night involved in a scam. The report will also tell you how long the company has been in business and who the principals are. It should also provide the legal name of the entity, which is important. If the credit application is filled out and signed in the incorrect name, you may find yourself with no legitimate business to go after if the invoice is not paid.

Verifying the Company

Small companies and those just starting out may not have credit reports. When trying to verify the business, do not use the phone numbers provided by the company. Look them up in the phone book or call information to get the information. Why? Check this information from third-party sources to avoid being taken by individuals looking to scam your company. The same is true when checking trade references. If the reference is from ABC Company, call information and get a phone listing for ABC Company. Then use the phone number provided by information to check the reference. Why? A fraudster may provide you with the name of a very impressive company for a reference but actually have a friend or associate provide the reference. If you call using the number provided, you will be connected to the accomplice rather than a legitimate reference.

Trade References

Before extending credit on open account terms, most companies will check trade references to see how the potential customer pays its bills. Typically, the potential customer will provide the names of the references, along with the phone numbers. Now, like most people, they will only provide the names of companies that will give good references.

Once the credit professional has contacted the trade reference using phone numbers obtained from information, he or she should try and ascertain other companies that the potential customer has done business with. Once the other companies have been identified, the credit professional can contact them, if possible. This needs to be done carefully. One of the best ways to find out about a potential customer is from credit industry groups. If you belong to such a group for your industry, check its latest reports to see how the potential customer has paid your peers.

Financial Statements

Financial statements are typically used to paint a picture of the financial health of the company. However, as credit professionals are well aware, numbers can sometimes be manipulated. Thus, it is important to have statements that are audited by an independent accounting firm. Financial statements come in three levels:

1. *Audited statements* are compiled by an independent accounting firm from company records. This is the preferred type of statement. The audit firm signs off on the statements when the audit is complete. They typically state that the accounting conforms to generally accepted accounting principles (GAAP). This is referred to as an *unqualified* and it is what credit managers ideally want to receive.

   If the accounting firm disagrees with the way the company handled one or more transactions believing the issue does not conform to GAAP, it will give a *qualified* statement. Companies generally will go to extreme lengths to make sure that their auditors give an unqualified statement as many believe a qualified statement is a sign of bigger problems. It can also trigger an investigation from parties such as the Securities and Exchange Commission (SEC)—something virtually every company would like to avoid.

2. *Reviewed statements* are what they indicate. The audit firm reviews the numbers put together by the client, but the accountants have not audited the company's procedures.

3. *Compiled statements* are put together on the basis of information provided by the company to the accountant. The accounting firm has no way of determining if the numbers are accurate or if the company has complied with GAAP.

Financial Statements—Age

The more current the statement, the more reliable the numbers will be to the credit manager using the information to complete a credit evaluation. Typically, the numbers may be as much as 18 months old. Here's why. The accountants only audit once a year and this is done after the fiscal year-end. Thus, already some of the information is a year out of date. Then the company must complete the audit and prepare the financial statements. This can and usually does take several months. However, new statements should be available six to nine months after the end of the fiscal year. If they are not, it could be a sign of financial difficulties.

Additionally, credit professionals are well advised to look twice at customers who change their fiscal year-end. Very rarely is there a good business reason for making the change, often the change is done to hide something. Thus, whenever a change is noted, question the customer for the reasoning behind the change.

What Is Included in Financial Statements?

Several important documents are included in the general term financial statements.

Income Statement. The income statement is the starting point for most credit investigations. It tells the profit-and-loss story for the current fiscal year. Examine the statement closely for any unusual or nonrecurring items, such as the sale of a facility, a change in accounting methods, a large tax credit, or a write-off. If you find such items, recalculate the income statement, and then redo your ratio analysis based on the new numbers. After all, if the only reason a company showed a profit was that it sold a piece of real estate, this is a one-time gain that is unlikely to happen again.

Once you have the new ratios, compare them to industry standards to see if they are normal for the industry. If they do not fall within the accepted ranges, you will have to find out why the ratios are off.

Also take a close look at the statement of stockholders' equity to see if there have been any significant changes for the period the income statement covers. Again, if there were big changes, such as the owners making a capital contribution or the sale of new stock, you need to determine the reason for the change.

Balance Sheet. The balance sheet, sometimes called the statement of financial condition, shows the financial condition of the company. It reflects both long- and short-term assets and liabilities.

Cash Flow Statement. Although traditionally the cash flow statement was not deemed to be that important, increasingly it is seen as vital to those analyzing the financial condition of a company. It shows the cash inflows and outflows of the customer. It is especially important to credit professionals who are very concerned about making sure the customer has adequate cash flow to pay all its short-term obligations, especially vendor obligations. Some even call cash flow the lifeblood of any organization. Anything that adversely affects it needs to be examined closely.

Footnotes. Some of the most important information about a company is hidden away in the footnotes. Long and complicated footnotes deserve extra attention. Again, they do not necessarily mean bad news, but they do need to be inspected closely. Additionally, they may provide invaluable information that is not included elsewhere in the financial statements. What kinds of information might you find? Details about lawsuits pending against the company, use of tax credits, the condition of the pension plan, and the status of leases and mortgages or deferred compensation commitments. Information about certain contingent liabilities will also be buried in the footnotes.

Most customers will not voluntarily offer this type of information to their creditors. You must find it. These facts can often have a negative bearing on a credit decision—provided you unearth them.

Ratio Analysis

It is recommended that trend analysis be used when evaluating the balance sheet, income statement, statement of cash flows, and ratios. Ideally, five years' worth of data should be used. *Trend analysis* is the comparing of key ratios from each year against industry norms to pinpoint movement toward improvement or decline in a business and to identify unusual items.

No ratio can be looked at in isolation. For example, most credit professional believe that a quick ratio of 1 is a good indication of a financially stable company, but it is important to do a little digging into that number. The quick ratio is defined as cash, marketable securities, and accounts receivable divided by current liabilities. If the company with a quick ratio of 1 also has a days sales outstanding of 65, when the industry norm is 45 that quick ratio no longer looks so good. There might be receivables that are not collectible. Thus, the quality of the accounts receivable must be good in order for that quick ratio to mean anything positive.

Listed below are the seven ratios credit professionals can use when evaluating unsecured trade creditors along with an indication of what the ratio signifies:

1. *Quick ratio* defines the degree to which a company's current liabilities are covered by the most liquid current assets.

2. *Days sales outstanding (DSO)* shows the average days it takes for the customer to collect its receivables.

3. *Accounts payable turnover* shows the average number of days that it takes the customer to collect its receivables.

4. *Inventory turnover* shows the average days that the customer takes to turn its inventory once.

5. *Debt to tangible net worth* indicates the ability of a firm to leverage itself. It shows how much the owners and creditors have invested in the firm. A high number reflects a potential danger to all creditors.

6. *Gross profit margin* is only meaningful when compared to the industry.

7. *Return on investment* reflects the efficiency of management's performance.

Caveats

Once these ratios are calculated for the time when the data is available (remember, five years is the best), the changes can be noted and a trend established. From that, it is possible to make a prediction and arrive at a credit limit. In making that decision, it is important that:

- The data be devoid of any large, unusual, nonrecurring items

- Any recent changes be incorporated into the data, such as a major acquisition, a bankruptcy filing, or a spin-off of a major product line

- The same formula that is standard in the industry be used

- Data be compared to others with the same Standard Industry Classification (SIC) codes and in similar narrow-dollar sales ranges

- Commonality in how industry numbers value inventory and how customers compute depreciation is uncovered. This can usually be found in the notes section of the annual report

- The footnotes in the annual report be checked carefully for unusual or one-time occurrences that will affect the company's results. Some companies have been known to bury unpleasant news and negative financial data in the footnotes. It is not unusual for such facts to be overlooked

Cash Burn Rate

What do you do when you're asked to extend credit to an Internet start-up? Most credit professionals realize that the traditional methods of analyzing a company will not work for their new Internet customers. Forget comparing data for the last five years—many of these companies have not been around long enough to have two years of audited financial statements.

First of all, refusing to grant credit on any terms other than cash in advance is probably a wise course. Few companies would stand for that, although it is not a bad idea in the case of truly shaky firms. Liquidity can be a real issue for Internet companies. Those who follow the financial and Internet news probably are accustomed to hearing the analysts talk about Internet companies running out of cash. Some refer to this as the cash burn rate or the cash burnout rate.

To calculate this number, add cash to marketable securities and accounts receivable (A/R). This number should be divided by daily operating expenses and then 365. This will give an indication of when your Internet customer could run out of cash. The answer to this calculation will guide you in the credit decision. It can also help to get management to see why you do not want to extend credit, if that is the case. A visual depiction of the cash burn rate is:

$$\frac{\text{Cash} + \text{A/R} + \text{Market Securities}}{(\text{Daily Operating Expenses})(365)}$$

Some credit professionals like the cash burn rate concept so much they have incorporated it into their financial analysis of existing customers.

Nonfinancial Factors That Affect the Credit Decision

As virtually every credit professional knows, making a credit decision is as much an art as it is a science. The stark financial analysis may indicate that the customer should not be granted credit terms, but there are often other factors to be considered. Here is a brief look at some of the nonfinancial issues that affect the final determination:

- *The 5 Cs of credit: character, capacity, capital, conditions, and collateral.* One credit analyst revealed that his company routinely sold on open-account terms to a customer, whose numbers were awful. The reason was simply that this company always paid its bills and was never late. "I'd rather deal with this customer any day," says the analyst, "than those large companies who continually string us along for payment even though they have the money."

- *Relationship with the buyer.* Oftentimes, if a long-term ongoing relationship with a customer exists, credit executives are more likely to allow the company to go over its credit limit. However, watch the payment patterns closely if this is allowed. Most credit professionals who follow this strategy do it with customers who have seasonal businesses.

- *The customer's payment history.* If it is good, some credit professionals are apt to be more aggressive in finding ways to grant open-account credit terms. However, if it has been bad, most in the group indicated that they would be inclined to reduce the credit line if the sales force didn't squawk too much.

- *Profit margin on the product in question.* Without a doubt, a company that sells products with tight margins were much less likely to be flexible when extending credit. "We just can't afford to be wrong," explains one weary credit professional. However, those with wide margins were more apt to stick their necks out a bit and extend credit.

- *Status of the product.* Is it already manufactured and sitting in the warehouse? If so, the sales force is likely to bring this to credit's attention, especially if the end of the season for the goods in question was approaching or if the product had been moving slowly. At this point, some credit professionals are more likely to get creative to find ways to make the sale happen.

- *Status of sales goals.* Is the sale needed to make the budget? Unfortunately, as the accounting period ends, many credit professionals find themselves being pressured to grant credit for sales that don't meet credit standards. Several report that this happens with greater frequency if sales goals are not met.

- *Role of sales.* Will sales be willing to get involved in collection efforts should the customer not pay? While most salespeople are reluctant to get involved with collection efforts, several of the credit professionals indicate that they are able to exact a promise to help in exchange for extending credit in marginal cases. However, most who were able to do this say that they did this mostly with customers who were late payers. The preference of the group was to tie the salesperson's commission to the payment of the accounts receivable but few are successful on that front.

- *Customer's cooperation.* Is it possible to obtain a partial payment up-front to cover costs? In cases where the credit of the customer is questionable and the margins on the product high, a number of credit professionals simply ask for cash in advance for the portion that relates to the out-of-pocket costs. Then if the final payment is not received, the company only loses its profits. This also demonstrates to the customer a willingness to work together. Several who have tried this approach with new customers say that they are ultimately able to convert these accounts into long-term quality customers.

- *Mean versus ends.* Can this sale be used to leverage payment on an outstanding order? There is nothing more frustrating to a credit professional than to be approached by a salesperson to extend additional credit to a customer who is already late paying other invoices. However, should the customer really want the goods, it may be possible to make the sale if the customer agrees to pay the outstanding invoices. Ideally, such a customer should not only pay the outstanding invoices but make a partial prepayment on the new order.

If, after taking all the factors discussed above into account, credit cannot be granted, credit professionals should look for another "creative" way to grant the credit even if the customer does not meet financial standards. Not only will the company get the sale and have a higher profit, the sales force will appreciate the efforts.

How Different Companies Review New Accounts

Not all companies review credit in exactly the same manner. Depending on the nature of the business, the corporate culture, the resources devoted to the credit review process, and the amount of credit granted with open terms, companies set credit review guidelines. The range of what is done is quite wide. The following list includes just a few of the ways companies evaluate credit.

- Every new customer must complete a credit application.
- Have credit policies and procedures in writing and have them approved by senior management. This approval helps the credit department should sales try and bend some of the rules.

14

- Call all new customers and explain discount terms. Encourage customers to call before taking any deduction.
- New credit applications are reviewed thoroughly and questionable accounts put on cash-on-delivery (COD).
- Use multiple sources of information, including the Internet, to obtain factual data on companies.
- Pull credit reports on new customers over the Internet, allowing quick turnaround on credit applications.
- Sales and credit review customer programs in detail. Profitability analysis, capacity, and other key factors are all part of the credit line granting process.
- Have the board of directors revise and clarify credit policy and terms.
- Divide the credit application into two parts: the credit agreement and the application for credit.
- Streamline the new account set-up process.
- Assign one person to set up new accounts, send out credit applications, and process them once they are completed and returned.
- Have all customers complete an application and a customer profile so the credit analyst can see the big picture.
- Redesign the credit application so it is easier to fill out. Eliminate any meaningless requirements and add slots for e-mail addresses and customer Web sites.
- Set up form letters on the personal computer (PC) to autofax for credit references.
- Require bank/trade references with completed credit application.
- Work with sales on the credit application process. Make sure they get a signed contract and authorization rather than just a verbal commitment.

- Make the credit approval for all new customers consistent. Require the same information from all before credit is granted. Once the process is standardized, the sales reps know what will be required and make sure the customers supply it.

- Automatically give new accounts a small credit line with minimal credit checking. Then reevaluate based on financial information and payment habits.

- Formalize a thorough process involving pulling credit reports, reviewing the customer's completed credit application, and accessing financial information over the Internet.

- Have a training program for the existing credit staff to make sure they all understand the nuances of credit and are using the same corporate standards.

- Hire a full-time credit administrator to monitor the credit-approval process.

Existing Accounts

Just because a rigorous credit evaluation was completed when a company first becomes a customer does not mean that analysis is good forever. Most experts recommend that credit reviews of all accounts be done at least once a year. However, the reality is that ongoing credit reviews are one of those things that get pushed back when the credit staff does not have enough time to do all the work that it has on its plate. *IOMA* statistics show that only about 50% of all companies review all accounts annually. This is too bad because long-term customers do run into financial difficulties and it would be nice if you were able to cut your firm's exposure before the customer can no longer pay. Here's a sampling of how some companies review the credit limits of their existing customers:

- Each month, the computer generates a list of all customers that are up for their annual review.

- Request updated financial statements from major accounts. Also pull updated D&B reports, and get trade credit reports from local trade groups.

- Review current credit limit and past payment history to determine if higher credit limits should be granted to each customer once a year.

- Review existing accounts with controller once a year and discuss the status of each.

- During the slow time, the top 75 customers are reviewed. For some companies the slow time is May, June, and July, but it may differ for other seasonal businesses.

- Depending on the level of activity in the account, each customer is reviewed annually or semi-annually.

- Only review the top 25 customers each year.

- Customers with large balances or changes in their payment habits are reviewed each year.

- Continually monitor largest customers. Any customer who has not done business with the company in over a year is forced to go through a new credit check.

- Accounts are all set up for annual review by placing an indicator in the sales system. The list is printed monthly and the accounts updated. Depending on the credit limit, the update may consist of obtaining new financial statements, updating credit reports, and trade and bank references.

- Have procedures in place to request financial statements annually. Input the follow-up information into a credit rating model. Those customers whose ratings come out poor or marginal are then reviewed in greater detail.

- Depending on the size of the company and whether it is private or public, the financial statements are reviewed, references are updated, and the past history with the company is reviewed. Credit limits are reset based on this evaluation.

- If a customer consistently bumps up against its credit limit but pays within acceptable limits, the limit is reviewed. If the payment history is not acceptable, "the whole enchilada" is done again.

- Accounts due for annual revision are compiled in a monthly report. An analyst uses the report to determine which accounts need to be reviewed.

- The credit manager and the assistant credit manager review customers' creditworthiness along with input from the salesperson.

- Pull simple Experian credit reports to show changes. Look at the payment record and sales levels to determine next action.

- Update data by mail and phone.

- Update information from the credit bureaus and National Association of Credit Managers (NACM) reports.

- Use credit scoring to determine which accounts get reviewed.

- Only review major accounts. Review annual reports and a three-year spreadsheet. Also discuss the customer at credit groups.

- Run reports to show which accounts have orders that will exceed their credit limits. These accounts are then reviewed.

- Evaluate current payment patterns, and update trade references and financial information for a formal review of the credit limit.

- New credit reports, financial information, and trade references are assembled. A log is kept of all files in review. A recap sheet is completed for management review. A last review date is updated in the computer.

- Only accounts with large credit lines are reviewed.

- Maintain a monthly analysis of all customer credit lines and sales and payment methods.

- Conduct a thorough analysis two to three times a year with upper management and monthly meetings with the department staff.

- Set a goal of having all accounts updated every 18 months. Get a monthly listing of all accounts that have not been updated within this time frame, and make sure an account's last review date shows on all accounts receivable screens.

- Review those accounts that are very active and purchase over $100,000 each year.

- For some companies, an annual credit review is an audit requirement. All accounts carry an annual review date, which posts automatically to an exception list. Every account is reviewed for performance and appropriate file support (latest trade and bank references, and so on).

- Set the system to flag any order that has not been reviewed for 12 months. Credit is notified and depending on the order value, the history is reviewed, a new credit report is pulled, and a decision is made to extend or change limits for the upcoming year.

- All credit managers review their areas of responsibility in total. Also, a credit check program alerts if a credit is more than 12 months old.

- Based on average accounts receivable balances, reviews are done quarterly, semi-annually, or annually. New financials and trade reports from industry groups are obtained. Any other information with the exception of new trade references is also acquired. If the customer is international, a country report is also pulled.

- Run customer profiles and go through an average days of payment to try and pinpoint potential trouble before it occurs.

- During the first quarter, accounts with limits over $25,000 are reviewed. In the second quarter, those with limits between $10,000 and $25,000 come under scrutiny. The third quarter is spent focusing on those with lower limits, and the fourth quarter is spent making sure that credit files for every active account are in place and updated.

Credit professionals should try to review existing accounts at least once a year not only because it is a good business practice but also to protect themselves. When the credit review is done, the documentation should be put in the file and any recommendations should also be filed. If management overrides you, it is imperative that at a minimum a note to this effect be put in the file. Ideally, the override would be in writing—but that is often difficult. The reasons for this are fairly simple. When one of these marginal accounts goes bankrupt and ends up owing your company thousands (or more) of dollars, management is going to point a

TIPS & TECHNIQUES

Watch Out for Large Exposures

When reviewing a potential customer's credit application, some credit professionals believe in looking at that customer's ten largest customers to see what the total exposure is. Be careful if one customer represents too large a percentage of your potential customer's business. If one of their large customers goes broke, there could be financial implications for your company. Think this can't happen? Just look at some of the big companies that have experienced financial difficulties and have even gone out of business. There was a time when Lucent was golden, but as this is being written Lucent is fighting for its financial life. Most companies limit their exposure to any one company to no more than 5 to 10% of their total business.

finger at credit and ask "why wasn't credit on the ball to see this trouble coming." If you have a notation in the file that you warned management and sales, and they decided to ignore your advice, you will avert the blame. They still won't be happy with you, but at least credit won't shoulder the full responsibility for the loss.

What Should Be in the Credit File?

When taking legal action because of nonpayment or bankruptcy of a customer, some credit managers find they do not have the information they need. If the facts and figures were not collected when the account was first opened, the customer will probably not provide them when the account gets into financial difficulty. This information is not difficult to obtain when the account is first set up. The customer is interested in putting on a good face with the vendor. While amassing these reports for each new customer may seem a waste of time, the credit professional will be paid back many times over for this effort when the account goes bad. So, exactly what should you keep in debtors' credit files? The following information comes from Creim, Macias & Koenig, LLP.

Basic Information

The data listed in this section are usually needed to prepare documents. While it seems elementary, some credit professionals report it missing from their files. It includes:

- The identity of the debtor, including its correct name, form of business, and whether it is one entity or multiple entities
- Locations of the debtor
- Locations of the debtor's assets
- Value of collateral
- Form of debt (invoices, statements of accounts, promissory notes)

Creditor Documents

"A credit application," says Bill Creim, one of the firm's partners, "is the one document the debtor signs, so include all areas where difficulties are likely to arise." He recommends including terms, conditions, and whether interest may be charged on late payments. He delineates the items that should be included in the file as follows:

- Credit applications, security agreements, dealer agreements or distributor agreements, sales contracts, guarantees, and other written correspondence showing

  - Interest

  - Attorney fees and collection costs

  - Acceleration

  - Debtor's books and records

  - Jurisdiction and venue clauses

  - Arbitration clauses

- Financial information including

  - D&B, Experian, or other credit reports

  - Audited financial statements

  - Unaudited financial statements

- Unmarked original documents and letters contained in credit manager's and salesperson's files

- Invoices and statements of account. Creim warns credit professionals to beware of usury problems, collection costs, and payment terms.

Other Sources of Information

In addition to the details listed above, miscellaneous intelligence—such as information from banks, other creditors, or competitors—should be

TIPS & TECHNIQUES

Checking Out New Customers

The old adage, "if something looks too good to be true, it probably is," is especially pertinent to credit professionals when they check trade references on new clients. A potential customer gives you the names of three companies and contacts there. You reach all the contacts, who respond that the customer pays bills on time and is no problem. What could be wrong with that? A lot, says D&B.

You should be suspicious if a reference uses only superlatives to describe the customer and doesn't need to look up the customer's records. Also think twice if a hard-to-trace fax number is the only way to reach a reference: You don't really know who'll receive the fax. Here are some suggestions from D&B on checking on references before you rely on them to support the potential customer:

- Check with the Yellow Pages or other outside sources to confirm that the reference company actually exists.

- Call information and ask for the phone number of the reference company. See if it's the same as the number the potential customer gave you.

- Make sure the person you speak to really works for the reference company and is in a position to speak for the company.

- Ask to speak to the credit manager instead of the person whose name was provided.

- Make sure the reference is in a business in which the customer could logically be expected to work.

Will these steps guarantee that a phony reference won't sneak past you? No, but following these simple procedures certainly will make it more difficult for someone trying to pass bogus references.

included. Creim warns credit professionals that they must make sure that nothing in the file could be misconstrued as slander or interference with normal business relationships. Credit professionals must also omit anything that might show antitrust violations.

Much of the material kept in the credit files needs to be updated regularly. New financial reports and sales contracts should routinely be included in the credit files. Similarly, new credit reports should be pulled periodically to make sure your customer's financial standing is as good as (or better than) it was when the account was first opened.

In the current environment, which Creim describes as "we cheat our suppliers and pass the savings on to you," it is imperative that credit professionals do everything to protect their companies against nonpayment.

Some companies actually have the information discussed above but cannot find it when it is needed. The importance of having all relevant documents in one place should not be underestimated.

IN THE REAL WORLD

The Credit Application...
Circa 1892

Speaking at the FCIB's Global Credit Conference, Credit2B.com's Al Carmenni shared some requirements he'd located on an 1892 credit application. That's right, he was in possession of a credit application that was over 100 years old. It had about 40 questions. Some focused on financial issues, as might be expected. However, the following, rarely found on credit applications today, caused the audience to laugh. The application inquired about the principals' drinking habits, wanted to know if the principals were racetrack followers, or if they were politicians.

Setting a Credit Limit

Most credit professionals believe that setting a credit limit is as much an art as it is a science. Some companies use a simplistic approach offering customers 10% of the customer's net worth capped at some level. For example, most vendors with annual sales of $100 million will never offer a customer a line of more than $10 million. The reason is simple —the vendor simply cannot handle the limit no matter how good the company, and it is also a very poor idea. Most companies like to limit their exposure to any one company, never allowing one company to represent more than 10% of its annual business.

Others use a formula based on the customer's financial numbers.

Warning Signs

Alert credit professionals will find signs of potential trouble in their day-to-day operations. The following are some signs that might signal trouble:

- A normally prompt paying customer begins to take longer and longer to pay its invoices.
- A small customer suddenly places a much larger order than normal.
- Other credit managers report late payments at industry group meetings.
- Sales finds a new customer that must have a large order quickly.
- A customer that took minimal deductions suddenly starts taking large deductions.

Types of Credit Report

When most people think of credit reports, they think of D&B reports. These reports contain much information that might be useful to credit professionals. Some in the field are less than impressed with D&B reports

—yet, despite the complaints, most credit professionals use D&B reports. The reports are good for verifying that the company exists. However, when it comes to financial analysis, do your own. Also, realize that the information is sometimes outdated.

The second runner-up in the credit-reporting field for businesses is Experian, formerly known as TRW. The company's reports are not used widely in the United States but have a wider exposure in Europe.

Other reports are available from NACM affiliates, Riemer, and other specialty credit associations.

International Customers

One of the biggest mistakes companies make when they first dip their toes into the international arena is to assume that business overseas runs the way it does in the United States. That simply is not the case and proceeding using that assumption is likely to get a company into big trouble.

The second biggest mistake made by more than a few companies is to throw credit considerations right out the window. These companies decide that evaluating international credit is very difficult and therefore they won't even bother. Thus, they end up granting credit to every customer that shows up including those that they would never offer open-account terms to had they been a domestic customer.

Selling to companies in other countries requires different approachs than when selling domestically. For an in-depth study, see *International Credit and Collections* (Schaeffer, New York: John Wiley & Sons, Inc., 2001).

Credit Software

To help with credit- and collection-related issues, many professionals use specialty credit software. It is used for credit analysis, scoring to help with collections, and a myriad of other credit-related issues. It is discussed in some detail in Chapter 11, which addresses technology issues.

Summary

As you can see, there isn't only one way to analyze credit. The approach selected by each company will match its industry needs along with the resources it is willing to devote to the credit process. By evaluating the discussion above and reviewing some of the techniques used by different companies, you will be able to devise the best credit approach for your company.

CHAPTER 2

The Second Step: Billing

After reading this chapter you will be able to

- Understand the implications of billing on business credit and collections
- Prepare a clear and accurate invoice that does not prevent your company from being paid in a timely manner
- Recognize the effect terms can have on collections
- Implement electronic billing in your organization

Often overlooked in the business cycle, the billing process, handled incorrectly or inefficiently, can cost a company thousands of dollars. Those credit professionals looking to improve their collection results should begin by looking at the billing process.

What Is An Invoice?

Simply put, an invoice is a bill. It provides the customer with the necessary information to pay for goods ordered and delivered. It should also include any other pertinent information needed to pay the invoice in a timely and precise manner.

When Should the Invoice Be Sent?

Invoices should be sent as soon as possible after the goods have been shipped. The reason for this is simple. Let's say your payment terms call for payment in 30 days. Most customers will start the clock counting from the time they receive the invoice. Thus, if you only send out invoices once a month, some customers may actually take 60 (or more) days to pay.

Now some reading this may declare that the terms are from the invoice date. However, that is not how most customers will count. Additionally, it takes most companies time to process invoices for payment. In many organizations, the invoice must be sent to the purchasing department for approval and then back to the accounts payable department for payment. These steps take time as approving an invoice is not typically a high priority. Also, the customer is in no hurry to make payment so the longer you delay in sending an invoice, the longer it will delay in making payment.

While printing invoices every day may not make sense for mid-size and smaller companies, once a month might not be an ideal solution either. Once or twice a week might be a reasonable approach.

Terms

The payment terms indicate when an invoice is supposed to be paid. Few organizations will pay early. Many will pay late. It is the goal of the credit department to get as many customers to pay as close to stated terms as possible. The most desirable terms are referred to as open account. This means the customer is given the goods and does not have to pay for them for some time. In many industries the terms are net 30. This means that the customer is expected to pay in 30 days. Here's where it gets a little vague. The seller wants the invoice paid within 30 days of the invoice date. However, most customers believe that the payment is due 30 days after receiving the invoice—hence the need to get the invoice out quickly.

Terms are generally dictated by industry. For example, the food industry tends to have shorter terms, say seven or ten days, while some machinery manufacturers might have longer terms, even as long as 180 days. Those selling internationally will find that most companies in other parts of the world are accustomed to longer terms, with 60 days and longer not being considered uncommon.

Sometimes, in order to induce early payment, companies offer a discount for quick payment. The much-fabled 2/10 net 30 is a common example. In this case, payment is expected in 30 days. However, if the customer will pay in ten days or less, it may take a 2% discount. While 2% may not seem like a big discount, it translates into an annual return of approximately 36%—a rate that few companies have earned in recent times.

The problem with offering discounts to induce early payment is that some customers take the discount but don't pay early. You will read much about the unearned discount problem in Chapters 3 through 5. It can be a huge problem for some companies.

Customers that don't qualify for open-account terms, either because their credit history doesn't warrant it, because their payment history is poor, or because they have not offered sufficient financial information or references can still be sold to. It can be done on a cash-in-advance (CIA) basis, a secured basis, or a cash-on-delivery (COD) basis. Secured selling will be discussed in Chapter 8. Cash in advance is preferable to COD because, as some companies have learned the hard way, COD has its pitfalls. Specifically:

- The person needed to sign the check may not be available when the driver shows up with the goods.
- No check is available when the goods are delivered.

- The customer changes its mind and does not offer payment when goods are delivered.
- The customer puts a stop payment on the check after it has accepted the goods.
- The check bounces after the goods have been delivered.
- The driver forgets to pick up the check when he delivers the goods.

Despite its drawbacks, COD is a viable option, especially when the amount of money is not large.

Due Date

As indicated above, customers generally start the clock ticking when the invoices arrive in their office. Sometimes they don't start counting until the invoice arrives in the accounts payable department. One way to get around this issue is to make the due date crystal clear on the invoice. This will not guarantee payment when you think you should get it, but it will eliminate confusion over the correct date.

How to Make the Invoice Date Clear

There are several ways to make the due date clear. Making the date clear is just the first step in getting paid on time. Several ways to make that date crystal clear to the customer's accounts payable department are to:

- Include the due date on the invoice. Don't leave it up to the customer to calculate the date. They will do the calculation to their benefit, not yours.
- Include a statement that says "Pay this invoice by…"
- Bold the due date.

Information That Should Be Included on Invoices

The following information should be included on invoices:

- Addressing: correct address, company, department, contact person
- Description of delivery, product/services, quantities, delivery location and date
- Clear specification of the amount, including possible supplements
- Reference or purchase order number of the other party
- Order date
- Person/department who did the ordering
- Clear statement of payment conditions
- Clear statement of the desired method of payment
- Name and direct dial number of the credit manager responsible

Are Your Invoices the Cause of Your Collection Woes?

After taking a long hard look at their invoices, a number of credit professionals have discovered that part of their collection problems were self-inflicted. By making sure that the invoice leaves nothing to the discretion or imagination of the customer, these credit professionals were able to plug some of their collection leaks. Credit professionals can take one of their invoices and pretend to be on the other side of the fence. Is the due date spelled out clearly, or is it left up to the customer to calculate it? If there are two ways to interpret the due date, you can be guaranteed that you will calculate it one way and your customer the other. Don't give your customer this opportunity. Print the due date on the invoice.

The same goes for the amount due. Do you leave it up to the customer to calculate the discount? Make it simple for them. State that x amount is due if the invoice is paid before date 1 and y amount if paid after. Also make sure the invoice is clear and the customer can find the

TIPS & TECHNIQUES

Other Invoice Tips

1 Don't print invoices on odd-colored paper. Many companies image invoices and you want to ensure that your invoices are easy to read.

2 Don't print invoices on odd-sized paper. Also, make sure the invoice is of decent size.

3 Make sure the printing on the invoice is clear and legible. Get rid of those old dot matrix printers.

4 Make sure the information on the invoice is clear and precise.

5 Include contact information so customers may contact the appropriate person if there is a problem.

6 Make the due date very clear.

7 While it is a good idea to review large dollar invoices for accuracy before sending to the customer, realize that you may be cutting into the discount period if early payment discounts are offered.

due date and amount due very easily. Where the check should be mailed to after it is drawn should be readily apparent. Many companies increase their float by simply mailing payments to the wrong part of the company. The check then spends a few days in interoffice mail. Finally, even though you have no real interest in increasing the number of calls coming into the department, put a name and phone number of the person responsible for resolving discrepancies on the invoice. By making it clear to the customer that you welcome phone calls, they may pick up the phone to resolve discrepancies instead of their calculators to do some creative accounting.

Best Billing Practices

Every industry has unique billing/payment issues. The publishing industry is no exception. In an attempt to set a standard for reasonable billing practices, the Magazine Publishers of America (MPA) set about to develop a Best Billing Practices Paper. Let me start out by telling you that this attempt did not make the publishers very popular with their customers—the large advertisers and the agencies that represent the advertisers. So, what seems like a very sensible project quickly turned controversial. Before casting stones at the agencies, it is necessary to understand their predicament. The following three problems only exacerbated the billing/payment issue:

1. Corporate payment stretching policies currently being used by many companies—including many advertisers who delayed paying their agencies

2. The agencies were then caught in a bind, not being able to pay the publishers until they had been paid by the advertisers.

3. Disputes

Publishers complained that frequently agencies would hold on to large payments when the disputed item was only a fraction of the total invoice. Was the dispute simply a ploy to avoid paying? To address the various problems, the Media Credit Association, a branch of the MPA, developed a draft proposal for industry best practices as they relate to billing and payment issues. Although the final paper was never formally adopted, you can learn from the Association's proposal and adopt its provisions in your own practices.

For those not familiar with the publishing industry, note that many publishers provide tear sheets of actual ads so the advertiser can verify that the advertisement actually ran. Can you imagine what a nightmare this can be for large publishers? Here is the MPA's proposal:

- Supply advertisers with either a complimentary copy or an affidavit to verify fulfillment. Ideally, as technology advances, digital images of advertisements could be used to verify fulfillment.

- Invoices will be prepared promptly and disputes communicated immediately—not after the payment is due.

- Payment terms are binding unless a deviation is agreed to in writing.

- Undisputed amounts will be paid in the agreed-upon time frame. Disputed amounts will be resolved quickly.

- The publisher has the right to notify the advertiser if the agency is more than five days late in paying the publisher. Agencies are not thrilled with this clause.

- Agree that old rates will be used while new contracts are being negotiated.

You can adopt some of the MPA's suggested best practices into your own billing procedures. Additionally, you should review your own industry peculiarities and find ways to incorporate these requirements into the invoice.

Electronic Billing

A paperless office has long been the dream of innovative, forward-thinking credit professionals. While it is not yet a reality, certain innovations are bringing this dream closer. Imaging and workflow technology were the first giant steps forward. Lately, there has been another innovation that could bring a paperless office within the reach of virtually every accounts receivable department, and make expensive imaging equipment obsolete in the process—electronic invoicing. Five companies spoke about the specifics of the products they offer (no two are identical) and about some of the obstacles billing and accounts receivable

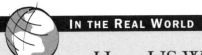
IN THE REAL WORLD

How US West Perfected
Its Billing Process

At a recent conference, Larry Rebenack, a director of the customer-billing department, explained how he combats the two issues of late and inaccurate invoices at US West.

Typical Problems

Once the invoice has been created accurately, it must be mailed expeditiously. Some of the mail problems that can slow its progress include having two different customers' data in the same envelope. How does this happen? Typical problems include:

- Having customer A's bill printed on one side, and customer B's bill printed on the back

- Having two different bill pages mingled together

- Having the bills cut wrong so that both customers' data are mixed in and mangled

Think this doesn't happen at your company? Talk to your mail center manager before dismissing such thoughts. Rebenack says that these *fatal* bills rack up costs to his company, because 40% of the time the customers call, with each call costing $50 to $100 to handle.

How to Fix It

In US West's case, several steps were taken to reduce the number of fatal bills. Several manual checks are made at the end of the print process to ensure proper printer placement and cutting, for example. Also, a manual inspection is made of the trayed mail, with two pieces from each tray pulled out and examined.

However, much of the error checking can be done electronically. To start with, there are electronic check characters on duplex printers, the cutting machine has gated sensors to ensure a proper cut of every document, and the mailing machine electronically verifies the barcode in the address window.

The "road to perfection" took US West four years, but the effects were dramatic. From March 1996 to 1997, there were 88,576 fatal bills at US West, according to Rebenack. From March 1997 to 1998, there were 577 fatal bills—only about 1% of all that were sent out. Between March 1998 and May 2000, there were no fatal bills.

Downstream Automation

Rapid automated bill payment processing also helped to reduce the defects in mail. It meant that the scanline had almost perfect readability and was in the correct position every time. The automated bill process barcoded every page, which made each bill easier to track along the way. *Corner marks,* little half-squares in the corner of the bills, visually verify the cut of the paper.

Reducing Problematic Return Mail

The mail center now monitors the return envelope drop rate, and reviews any maintenance problem associated with the rate. A vendor quality program also reduced the amount of problematic reply mail. That is, envelope vendors are expected to provide defect-free products, just as the mail center is, and are held accountable if something is wrong with their product or services.

The company also adopted a quality *process.* For one thing, the process included implementing an easy-to-read duplex multipaneled bill format. In other words, the printers now create bills that are easier to read, which not only help the customers, but allow staffers to quickly notice errors in a spot-check.

Other Tips to Improve Invoice Accuracy

Additional tips for improving invoice accuracy include:

- Be aggressive about correcting addresses.

IN THE REAL WORLD CONTINUED

- Track all bills during processing, to verify that a bill was actually mailed.

- Use one paper size for all types of invoices.

By following Rebanack's lead and working closely with their own mail center managers, credit professionals will be able to improve their own billing process.

---

professionals run into when they try to implement electronic invoicing. These are only a sampling of the offerings currently on the market.

Electronic invoicing is the delivery of invoices, most likely over the Internet, to a customer's accounts payable department in electronic format. No paper is received—although the invoice can be printed at any time—and the accounts payable department can then forward the invoice, via e-mail, to whoever needs to approve it. The information is then also available, without further keying, to be housed on a network for data retrieval. If it is combined with electronic payments, the information is then forwarded back (without rekeying!) to the vendor.

Why Is Electronic Invoicing Attractive?

In addition to the elimination of mountains of paper, accounts receivable professionals like electronic invoicing because:

- It eliminates mistakes due to rekeyed information.

- There are currently fears about the mail.

- It makes the workflow to route invoices for approval a no-brainer.

- It reduces costs.

- It makes it difficult, if not impossible, for others to blame the mail for their own shortcomings in processing paper.

Usage

If this is such a great deal, why aren't companies signing up en masse? We wondered the same thing and asked the product sponsors. The obstacles include:

- Cost
- Implementation time
- Budget constraints
- Internal resistance to change
- Lack of ease of use
- Difficulty in signing up partners
- Fear

Overcoming the Obstacles

Accounts receivable professionals who can determine why their companies and their customers are holding back are in the best position to offer a counterargument for why electronic invoicing is the right choice. The recent anthrax scares with the mail may provide the impetus needed for some companies to take the electronic billing plunge—although to date none of the companies interviewed have seen an increase in activity due to mail concerns.

If budget constraints or cost are issues, iPayables' Kim Rawlings suggests presenting "compelling return-on-investment data to build the business case for the initiative." He is happy to help credit professionals interested in his product make the case. BillingZone recommends the same approach. Its representative points out that Electronic Invoice Presentment & Payment (EIPP) offers both billers and payers a significant value proposition by eliminating paper from the process. It suggests that improved customer service, cash management, and accuracy in tracking and taking discounts are added benefits that can be factored into the equation.

Those facing the anonymous complaints of "it will take too long" or "our customers won't use it" should rely on documentation provided by the service provider. "We lay out a well-defined process and work with clients to ensure that the project is managed," says Open Business Exchange's Martha Perlin. Many of these vague complaints vanish when people understand what is expected of them and how the electronic invoicing process will work.

Fear of the unknown is a concept many accounts receivable professionals have encountered when trying to implement a new process. It is also what many are finding when they mention electronic invoicing in their own shops. "Validating the concept is probably the lengthiest process involved to garner buy-in from companies as a whole," points out Direct Commerce's Lisa Sconyers. "Such an application offers big money savings opportunities as well as extreme process streamlining, but our current economic market has instilled fear and conservatism toward implementing new technology," she concludes.

Sconyers has a few recommendations for credit professionals who find themselves facing this dilemma. She suggests they begin by calling and getting a referral from a customer already using the product. She points out that since her company can quickly and efficiently configure and integrate its application in a matter of days, a pilot program will give potential clients the opportunity to test the product firsthand at no risk.

Selecting the Best Service

A company interested in pursuing the e-invoicing route will base its own decision on its:

- Existing internal processes
- Budget
- Corporate culture
- Willingness to mandate change both internally and externally

Check out the Web sites or contact those vendors whose products interest you. Although e-invoicing may seem like a leading-edge approach today, in just a few short years it will be commonplace. Remember when the use of p-cards was considered innovative?

IN THE REAL WORLD

Specifics of
Five E-invoicing Services

❶ Name: Xign Collector

Company: The Xign Payment Services Network (XPSN)

Description: Suppliers submit invoices through electronic file upload or facilitated Web template entry. Buyers configure settings and rules for optimal processing of electronic invoices, including automation of data validation, posting, prioritization, routing, and approval (subject to buyer rules).

Both parties track status online from submission through receipt of payment.

Cost: Both buyers and suppliers pay fees for the services delivered to them. Pricing varies in proportion to the client's transaction volumes and to the benefit delivered. Buyers pay an annual subscription fee based on usage volumes. Suppliers pay a modest registration fee and transaction charges based on a percentage of savings from electronic processing.

Advantages:

- Accelerates collection and resolution of disputed payment items

- Online status tracking from invoice submission through settlement

- Unlimited remittance data in any format

- Simple, fast, electronic invoice submission

- Immediate identification of data and PO match exceptions

- Pinpoint accurate cash receipt forecasting

- Self-maintained directory information

- Simple to implement

- Complete online audit trail

Web site: www.xign.com

Contact Info: info@xign.com

(Source: *Xign*)

❷ Name: OB10

Company: Open Business Exchange

Description: OB10 is a secure system that facilitates the delivery of invoices between trading partners. Each buyer and its vendors can choose the most appropriate data format, standard, and means of communication. Using sophisticated data-mapping technology, we transform and deliver *any* invoice from any vendor to any buyer.

Cost: *For buyer:*

- Setup fee: $20,000 per accounting system/ERP

- Annual subscription: $10,000

- Volume-based pricing per invoice will average $0.25 to $0.75, depending on volume.

- Charges for optional services by invoice or unit

For vendor with accounting system:

- No setup fee

- Annual subscription: $750

IN THE REAL WORLD CONTINUED

- Pricing will average $0.25 to $1.00, depending on volume.

- Charges for optional services by invoice or unit

For vendor with no accounting system/using OBE's Web-based invoice creation and delivery:

- Annual flat fee dependent on volume, with a maximum of $100 per year.

- No charge for vendors with 12 or fewer invoices per year

Advantages:

- Buyer-driven solution

- No software or hardware installation

- Independent of formats or standards

- Short implementation time frames

- Quick return on investment

- Benefits to vendors as well as buyers

- Solution accommodates all vendor types

- Secure data storage

- Full audit trail available to reduce disputes and expedite resolution

Web site: www.obexchange.com

Contact Info: martha.perlin@obexchange.com or 212-828-2147

(Source: *Open Business Exchange*)

❸ **Name:** Direct Invoicing

Company: Direct Commerce

Description: DCI automates manual, tedious, and error-prone processes between accounts payable departments and their vendors. It provides services to:

IN THE REAL WORLD CONTINUED

Description: DCI automates manual, tedious, and error-prone processes between accounts payable departments and their vendors. It provides services to:

- Accept electronic invoices

- Deliver purchase orders

- Validate documents according to business rules and purchase order information

- Translate between different formats

- Allow vendors to perform inquiries

- Notify vendors of payments and other invoice status changes

- Facilitate dialogue and dispute resolution

- Route invoices for encoding and approval within organizations

Cost: Though both buyers and their vendors derive significant benefits from the Direct Commerce services, the fees are paid by the buying organization because they are the recipients of the tremendous cost savings. Its pricing is based on a transaction fee, which typically falls into the range of $2 per invoice.

Advantages: It offers more than just the electronic delivery of invoices and purchase orders, it actually manages the functionality and translates the information of the documentation within the processing of the invoice and purchase order (including workflow, matching, data validation, approval escalation). This allows for two-way straight-through processing and accurate information translation between two organizations.

Web site: www.directcommerce.com

Contact Info: Lisa Sconyers 415.288.9701 or lsconyers@directcommerce.com

(Source: *Direct Commerce*)

IN THE REAL WORLD CONTINUED

④ Name: BillingZone.com™

Company: Billing Zone

Description: BillingZone.com's EIPP service facilitates business-to-business transactions between billers and their payers. BillingZone.com is a simple way to present and pay invoices online and makes the management of complex workflow issues such as invoice routing easy. Payers can receive invoices from multiple billers on a single Web site to review, schedule, dispute, and pay invoices.

Cost: BillingZone's fee structure is based on a one-time implementation fee and transaction fees. It offers solutions to both billers and payers with fees based on the complexity of the implementation and the invoices themselves. Its typical implementation fee is less than $100,000. Many companies have paid less than this amount.

Advantages:

- Consolidated solution for billers and payers
- It is a service, not software.
- It is bank neutral, not requiring any banking changes.
- It is payer-focused.

Web site: www.billingzone.com

Contact info: info@billingzone.com or 877-965-4583

(Source: *BillingZone*)

⑤ Name: InvoiceWorks™ and ClearGear™

Company: iPayables

Description: By allowing vendors to key or upload invoice information via the Internet, iPayables eliminates paper from the invoicing process. iPayables makes it possible for invoice payers to receive invoices electronically from all vendors and suppliers regardless of their size or technical ability. The InvoiceWorks™ and ClearGear™ applications allow easy routing, approval, and delivery of invoices from vendors and suppliers to payer's accounts payable systems.

Cost: Initial setup and implementation is less than $100,000. Per-invoice transaction fee of $1.45 or lower depending on invoice volume. Annual maintenance is $15,000. All paid by clients. No charge to vendor/supplier to use service.

Advantages:

- Reduce invoice-processing cost by 70% to 90%
- Strengthen vendor relationships
- Eliminate data entry
- Reduce processing time from days and weeks to minutes
- Detailed history and audit trail
- Eliminate lost invoices
- Reduce clerical staff by 30% to 50% and reassign existing staff
- Keep labor costs under control
- Dramatically reduce vendor inquiry calls through online tracking and status
- Capture more negotiated term discounts
- Eliminate keying errors
- Reduce discrepancies, costs, and processing time

Web site: www.ipayables.com

Contact Info: kim.rawlings@ipayables.com or 877-774-7932

(Source: *iPayables*)

Summary

Billing is an important function that affects the bottom line. If done as efficiently as possible, collections will come in faster increasing investment income or decreasing borrowing expenses. It is a function that is often overlooked when companies are looking for ways to become more efficient. Thus, by making recommendations for change in this area, credit professionals can make a difference.

As companies continue to look for ways to cut costs and become more efficient, electronic billing will become a more common tool in corporate America. Those who understand what is involved will be well armed to advise their companies.

CHAPTER 3

The Third Step: Collecting the Money

After reading this chapter you will be able to

- Understand where collections fits into the big picture
- Evaluate different collection techniques
- Know when to turn an account over to a collection agency
- Realize when a lawyer is needed to approach the debtor

There is an old saying in the credit profession that says, "a sale is a gift until the invoice is paid." It is the job of the collectors to turn those gifts into sales. If customers paid what they owe when it was due, there would be no collection jobs. However, as those involved in the field are well aware, not only are companies not paying their bills on time, there is a growing trend toward paying them later and later. Thus, the need for collectors with good skills is stronger than ever.

There are a wide variety of approaches that can be taken to collect money and collect it faster. The traditional collection tool was a letter. While this is still used, and we'll share some collection letter techniques that work, many look down on this approach. The phone is the approach that many deem the most successful for generating payments. In this electronic age, fax machines and e-mail are also used. This chapter breaks down collection advice into these groupings along with offering some general advice and some techniques to use to get the sales force to help. Finally, we will also share a few other approaches that collection professionals have used with success.

General Advice

Many credit professionals believe that the collection process begins when the credit application is first taken. By spelling out in the credit application the terms of sale and any penalties that may accrue due to late payment, credit professionals are laying the groundwork for their collection efforts. While there are many different ways to go about collecting, some of the suggestions fall under the classification of general as they apply to more than one area.

TIPS & TECHNIQUES

Collection Tips from the Field: General

- Anticipate, wherever possible, the customer's needs.

- Become best friends with the accounts payable manager at the corporate headquarters.

- Become a squeaky wheel with your largest delinquent customers. Let them know that you have no intention of going away until you have been paid. This will help with the current collection and future ones, as well.

- Become the squeaky wheel who gets paid first.

- Begin follow-up efforts earlier.

- Build a strong relationship with your customer's accounts payable manager.

- Communicate immediately with a past-due customer via an invoice copy and a computer-generated message. Follow this up with a phone call.

TIPS & TECHNIQUES CONTINUED

- Educate your customers. Make sure they know what your payment terms are and when you expect to be paid.

- Establish consistency in customer contacts. This means that credit, customer service, and sales must tell the customer the same thing when it comes to payment terms.

- Focus on largest accounts and get them to pay close to terms without letting the smaller accounts get completely out of hand.

- Follow-up, follow-up, follow-up. Use frequent and persistent phone calls to follow up on late payments.

- Get to know the accounts payable manager at your customer's company personally. If the manager likes you, your chances of getting paid on time will improve.

- Have a well-documented sales agreement defining payment expectations.

- Have collectors keep detailed notes of all promises made and follow up with customers the moment a promise is broken.

- Have invoices printed and mailed quickly. Some companies take a week or more to get invoices in the mail, and their customers start the clock running when the invoice hits their desks—not on the invoice date.

- Identify recurring problems with a particular customer and get involved in resolving the problem—even if it is something outside the credit and collection department.

- If your collectors run into the same problem with different companies, review your own internal procedures to see if you can fix the problem.

- Improve the collection staff's negotiating skills to improve the effectiveness and quality of customer collection calls.

- Make sure that your invoices are correct the first time they are printed. With accurate data, your customer will not have to waste valuable collection time trying to correct the invoice.

- Notify both the customer and the salesperson the minute an account is put on credit hold.

- Personal contact in a nonoffensive manner works well. Friendly reminders keep the communication channels open.

- Put some muscle behind your calls. If the customer doesn't do as it promised, follow up with the agreed-upon action. This will let them know in the future that you will act if they don't perform.

- Keep regular, consistent contact with customers' accounts payable personnel.

- Remember to say thank you. Phone, fax, or mail a small thank-you note to someone who has helped you resolve a problem. Once or twice a year, send a thank-you gift (such as a T-shirt or coffee mug) to everyone. This mass mailing will be more appreciated by the recipients if it is not done at year-end when other year-end gifts and festivities may diminish its value.

- Resolve all disputed issues before the due date of the invoice.

- Set deadlines and then communicate those deadlines both to those involved internally and to the customer.

- Support the customers' accounts payable staff in their efforts to resolve problems and discrepancies.

- Train the customers from the inception of the relationship. Explain due dates and collection policies to new customers as soon as the first payment becomes one day past due.

- Treat all people with respect. The customers do not look forward to the collections call, and letting them know their business is appreciated is a good way to start the conversation. Once the funds have been received, the hard decisions can be made.

- Use friendliness to disarm even the most cantankerous accounts payable manager.

- Use imaging for document retrieval. This will save your collectors an enormous amount of time by giving them the information they need without them having to pore over file cabinets to retrieve it and then refile it.

- Use technology, specifically faxes and e-mail to reach delinquent customers.

- With new accounts, especially if significant amounts are involved, make it clear that prompt payment is expected. If the customer is slow, tactfully jump all over it.

Using Snail Mail

Letters are the traditional collection tool. Many professionals don't like them because they claim they are ineffective. They claim that the customer recognizes the mailings and often doesn't even open the letter. If the customer does open the letter, they often discard it without reading more than the first few lines. Worse, the customer gets to know your collection letter cycle and how long it can go before you will cut them off. For example, a company might have a series of three or more collection letters, each increasing in the tone of the demand. If the customer figures out your sequence, and many will, they will know at exactly what point to pay. Thus, if you insist on using letters, don't stick to the same schedule. Don't make the letters too long and make sure they are addressed to the appropriate person. Yet, despite all the negative feedback about letters, many still use them. The following tips come from professionals in the field who successfully use letters as part of their collection program.

The credit community contains a small group of staunch advocates of letter writing for collection purposes. While others may think that letters are an ineffective collection technique, the steadfast group that uses them is able to quite successfully collect money that is owed using them. Some guidelines for successful collection letter writing are:

- Follow the KISS approach—Keep It Short and Simple.

- Keep the paragraphs and sentences short, making the letter easy to read and understand.

- Be specific about why you are writing and what you want.

- If at all possible, be positive—not easy when you are asking for money. You could start by saying your company values the customer's business.

- Send the letter to the correct person—someone who has the authority to make a payment decision.

- Be firm and fair and provide contact information so the customer can call to resolve any problems. At a minimum, this should include a name, phone number, and e-mail address. Make it as easy as possible for the customer to contact you.

- Never threaten action you are not prepared to take. Don't threaten to sue unless you intend to follow through.

- Design a series of letters, each more demanding than the former.

- Some suggest marking the envelope personal or confidential.

- Request address correction from the post office if letter cannot be delivered. Mark all envelopes address correction requested. This will help locate those who have skipped town without providing a forwarding address.

- Change your letters frequently—both style and format so your customers do not know what to expect from you as far as collections are concerned.

- If you suspect that your letters are not being opened, use a window envelope—the debtor may think the letter contains a check. While this approach does not guarantee a payment, it does pretty much increase your odds of getting the letter opened.

- Some collection professionals mark the envelopes that contain their collection letters past due to get the debtor's attention.

- Offer the customer a good reason to pay, something that will appeal to the "what's in it for me" thinking of the customers. These might include maintaining a good credit rating, not having its account put on credit hold, and so on.

Using the Fax Machine for Collections

The development of the fax machine put a new tool in the hands of the collection professional. It gives them the ability to put a collection

TIPS & TECHNIQUES

Collection Tips from the Field: Letters

- Adopt an aggressive letter campaign. Well-written letters can be more effective than a phone call with some customers.

- Give customers your self-addressed return FedEx airborne labels for large invoices. The definition of large will vary from company to company. Your company will not be charged for the mailing until the label is used.

- Redesign collection letters shortening the number of letters sent and the time between each letter.

- Review existing collection letters and rewrite if they are not firm enough.

- Send a "thank-you for your business" letter to each customer. Include on the letter a total of outstanding charges.

TIPS & TECHNIQUES CONTINUED

Some customers will pay their bill when the letter is received—even if it arrives before the invoice.

- Send a collection letter requiring half the owed amount within two weeks and the remainder within the following two weeks. Explain that if payment is not received, management reserves the right to review the case and take future legal action at its discretion.

- Send a letter to all new accounts outlining the credit terms. This notice should also be sent to reactivated accounts, so there can be no misunderstanding as to when payment is expected.

- Send a note to delinquent customers saying that they are exceeding their credit limit and will need to fill out a new credit application. Most customers do not want to fill out a new application and will simply bring their balance current.

- Send a strong ten-day demand letter indicating that the account will be turned over for collection and detailing collection fees the customer will be liable for. Seeing the additional 25% that the customer will be liable for seems to provide the necessary impetus to get the checkbook and pen out.

- Send a thank-you note to those customers who follow through on their promises.

- Send early notice letters for large dollar payments.

- Send letters to borderline accounts warning them that they will be cut off if the invoices go unpaid.

- Send reminder letters with a copy of the invoice.

- Send statements at the middle of the month so they don't get lost in the shuffle at month-end with all the other statements.

TIPS & TECHNIQUES CONTINUED

- To be taken seriously, send the follow-up letter by registered mail.

- To instill a sense of urgency in those customers giving you the runaround, send a ten day demand letter.

- When the customer is five days past due, send a follow-up memo. If the invoice goes unpaid for another 30 days, follow-up with a copy of the invoice, a proof of delivery, and a phone call.

letter or invoice in the hands of the customer almost instantaneously. To make the best use of this tool, make sure the fax is addressed to the appropriate party. Sending a collection letter, addressed to no one in particular, is a waste of time and effort. The fax will sit in the fax machine and eventually be thrown out.

Faxes can be used in another extremely successful way if your fax machine has the ability to auto fax and your collectors have online access to the company's invoices. When the customer claims it never received the invoice, the collector can simply ask for the fax number and with a few clicks of the mouse have the invoice on the way to the customer. While this may seem to be the ideal solution to this age-old problem, be aware that many companies will insist on an original invoice in order to make a payment. Many refuse to pay from fax copies. The official reason is that duplicate payments often arise when payments are made from copies or faxes. In all fairness to the other side, duplicate payments are a serious problem at many companies. However, that should not stop collectors from aggressively trying to get the customer who claims to have never received an invoice to accept a fax copy.

TIPS & TECHNIQUES

Collection Tips
from the Field: Faxes

- Fax a detailed statement at the beginning of each month to the specified person. Make a follow-up phone call to verify receipt of the fax and balance expected. At this stage, a payment plan can be worked out if one is needed.

- Fax copies of invoices to all customers who claim not to have received them.

- Fax customers past-due invoices with personalized hand-written notes on the invoice.

- Fax invoices instead of mailing them. This gets them in the hands of those who need them quicker. However, before implementing such a strategy, find out if your customer has a policy that prohibits paying from faxes. Some companies do.

- Fax statements and copies of invoices. This avoids the "I don't have the invoice" excuse and the fax keeps the item from going unnoticed.

- Fax the customers details of older unpaid invoices.

- Fax, fax, fax. Set up a form letter to fax past-due customers and attach a copy of the outstanding invoice(s) to it.

- Make your collectors more efficient. Put copies of the invoices on your system and give your collectors the ability to auto-fax them. Then, when a customer claims to have never received an invoice, they can send one with a few clicks of their mouse.

- Send a quick fax at 30 days instead of playing phone tag with customers you cannot reach. If they have voice mail, leave a message instructing them to check for the fax.

Using E-mail to Enhance Collection Results

E-mail is a wonderful way to communicate with others. If used judiciously, it can work wonders. Many of the suggestions that relate to snail mail are appropriate to e-mail. One of the dirty little secrets in corporate America is that a good number of professionals don't read most of their e-mail—so don't rely on this wonderful invention to solve 100% of your collection problems. Many people, myself included, automatically delete what they view as junk e-mail. Some use filters to weed out those annoying offers that seem to pop up out of nowhere. Be aware that using $$$ in the subject field is likely to get your message dumped in the junk e-mail folder.

E-mail provides an opportunity not available in other collection techniques—the subject field. Use that opening to catch your customers' attention. However, don't write something that might make the recipient think the message is junk.

TIPS & TECHNIQUES

Collection Tips from the Field: E-mail

- Send a follow-up e-mail including copies of the invoice or statements negating the requests for additional documentation.

- Try sending reminder notices via e-mail if you have an address.

- When sending an e-mail, try and develop a catchy phrase for the subject field. You want the recipient to open the message, not delete it. We are not suggesting you put a misleading statement in the subject line.

Phoning for Dollars

Many collection professionals believe that the phone is the best way to collect. Dialing for dollars is the way most companies chase their delinquent customers. Obviously, good phone etiquette is required. Some guidelines for making effective collection calls are:

- Prepare before the call. Have all the facts in hand before you dial the phone.

- Before making the call, review past collection history and promises—Is there a trend? Is it negative? Does the customer have a history of promising anything just to get the collector off the phone? If so, be prepared when the customer makes a seemingly positive promise.

- Make sure you get the correct person on the phone before going into your collection spiel. There is no reason to waste precious time with someone who cannot help you solve your collection issue.

- Identify yourself and the reason for your call immediately. Once you have the right person, get to the point.

- Don't do all the talking. When you've stated your case, stop. Wait for the customer to respond—"the pregnant pause." If there is silence, so be it. Don't rush in to fill it as many are apt to do whenever there is a lull in the conversation.

- Ask open-ended questions.

- Keep notes of all promises made and follow up immediately if they are broken. Let the customers know that they cannot get rid of you easily.

- Listen.

- Research and resolve all disputes quickly. Sometimes customers use minor discrepancies to avoid paying a large invoice.

- Always ask for payment in full.

- Confirm all agreements made during the phone call before hanging up. By doing this, you ensure that the customer is on the same page.

- Document everything meticulously.

TIPS & TECHNIQUES

Collection Tips from the Field: Phone

- Call as soon as the payment becomes past due and then follow up with additional phone calls every three or four days until the payment is received.

- Call before the invoice is due to let the customer know that the account is being watched and the payment is expected. At this time, you can also inquire about any problems that will delay payment.

- Call customers a few days before the due date to make sure they have all the information they need to make the payment. Discrepancies and disputes can be resolved at this time.

- Call customers who are known problems early in the process and verify that the invoice was received and that there are no problems that will delay payment.

- Call the customer before the invoice is due and make sure that there are no problems with the invoice.

- Develop a strategy for calling late-paying customers. Stick to it and meticulously follow up on all promises made.

- Have an organized collection process of telephone calling with an organized and timely follow-up on all commitments made.

- Keep a list of your worst offenders. Start calling them a week earlier than you usually do.

- Make a customer service call on the thirtieth day to make sure everything is all right and there are no unresolved disputes.

- Make sure your collectors have received adequate training on proper telephone techniques. Periodically, role-play to see if you can devise better ways of communicating with your customers.

- Place first collection call five days sooner than your current process and hold firm on a company policy of no shipments to any account that is more than 60 days past due.

- Set follow-up calls using an automated system such as GetPaid.

- Start the collection calling process with those accounts that owe the largest amount of money rather than those that are the oldest. This will make the most effective use of your collectors, especially if it is not possible for them to make all the calls you would like.

- Take full advantage of technology to help you get the most for your dialing dollar. Call customers with the largest outstanding balances first, rather than going after the oldest account that may have a small balance. Customers with balances that are very much past due should be cut off—even if the balance is small.

- Through verbal communication and follow-up calls, train the customer to have good paying habits—at least where your company is involved.

- When payment arrangements are made, call on the day the payment is due, not several days later. Be firm in a customer service fashion when making your collections calls. This approach may require some additional training for a staff that is not accustomed to taking this type of an approach.

As a last resort, if you can't get the debtor on the phone during normal business hours, try calling before 9 A.M. or after 5 P.M.

Getting the Sales Force to Help with the Collection Efforts

Even though most salespeople are loath to assist in collection efforts, some do and some do quite successfully. Often, the level of their success depends on how closely their compensation is tied to the collection efforts and accounts receivable aging.

TIPS & TECHNIQUES

Collection Tips from the Field: Sales

- Attend your company's sales meetings and address the sales force. Explain to them the company policy regarding timing of payment and answer any questions.

- Offer an award to the salesperson whose accounts have the best days sales outstanding (DSO).

- Produce a "Hall of Shame" list of delinquent customers by salesperson. Circulate the list to all salespeople.

- Provide each salesperson with a report showing the delinquencies on his or her accounts. Let them know which accounts are close to being cut off. Rather than lose an account, most salespeople will, however reluctantly, get involved with the collection effort.

- Set up a periodic meeting with the head of the sales department to discuss problem accounts and collection difficulties.

- Take back commissions associated with receivables that are more than 90 days past due. Some companies that are not willing to tie sales to commissions are willing to deduct

TIPS & TECHNIQUES CONTINUED

paid commissions if the receivable goes more than 90 (or some other agreed-upon number) days past due.

- Talk to the sales force and make sure all members understand that it is unacceptable to tell any customer that it is okay to pay late.

- Train the sales staff to make collection calls.

- When you are forced to put a customer on credit hold because of nonpayment, inform the appropriate salesperson and have that person apply a bit of not-so-subtle pressure. Have the salesperson place a courtesy call to the purchasing agent at that company and notify him of the credit hold. Then sit back and watch the sparks fly.

- Withhold salespeople's commissions until payments are received. This provides the sales force with the necessary incentive to help with collection activity.

Do Late Fees Help?

Business credit managers, anxious to find ways to get their customers to pay on time, are turning to a technique primarily associated with consumer collections—charging late fees. The practice, once shunned as unseemly in the business arena, is gaining converts, but what are the benefits and does it work? To assess the practicality of the late-fee approach, we talked with several credit professionals who have gone down this road as well as the Credit Research Foundation (CRF). The CRF shared the results of a recent late payment survey it conducted of its members.

Benefits and Drawbacks

The obvious advantage to charging a late fee is that it forces the customer to modify its behavior and begin paying its bills on time. Even if that does not occur, should you actually collect the late fee (more on this later), the income generated will at least partially offset the lost investment income (or increased borrowing costs) associated with the late payment.

While it may seem that late fees can only be a plus for the creditor, those who have charged them will attest that there are downsides to them. For starters, companies charging late fees run the very real risk of offending the customer. An offended customer generally translates into an angry salesperson—something most credit professionals have had more than their fill of. Then there is the administrative issue. "The hassle associated with the late fees far exceeds the small financial gain we've added to our bottom line," says one disheartened collection supervisor.

Who Gets Charged Late Fees?

The CRF survey shows that even those companies that assess late fees (35% of the survey respondents) do so sparingly. Slightly more than one quarter (27.2%) of those using late fees hit all their customers. The rest do so sporadically. When exceptions to the late-fee policy are granted, credit professionals will be happy to know that over two-thirds of the time, the decision to allow the exclusion is made in the credit department. The other times the decision is made as follows:

- 9.0% by sales
- 3.3% by marketing
- 12.3% by a senior executive

What is interesting to note is that although only one-third of the companies surveyed actually assess late fees, 86% say that their company's credit application includes a stipulation that indicates that the firm has the right to assess late fees on past-due accounts. When notifying customers of late payment charge policies, respondents to the CRF survey indicated that they use the following documents:

- Credit application (28.7%)
- Terms of sale agreement (20.8%)
- Invoice (27.1%)
- Statements (21.8%)
- Other (7.6%)

Methodology for the Assessment

Credit and collection professionals assess late fees in one of two ways. The most popular method is accruing the amount each month and adding it to the customer's account. This approach is used by 58.8% of those surveyed by the CRF. The remaining 41.2% invoice separately for the late fee.

While almost 70% stipulate the point at which they begin to assess the late payment fees in their late payment charge policy, not everyone sticks to the policy. In fact, almost half of the respondents (47.4%) indicated to the CRF that they did not strictly adhere to their stated policy.

While over half the respondents (53.3%) do not begin assessing late fees until the account is over 30 days past due, others start sooner. It should be noted that 28.7% of those surveyed do not carry the late fee on the accounts receivable account, but rather in a memo item off the books.

What about Robinson-Patman?

Many reading this are probably wondering if the ways that some companies apply late fees violates the Robinson-Patman Act. As credit managers are well aware, this Act requires that all companies in the same class be treated the same—as if there is no discriminatory pricing. "The good news about violating Robinson-Patman," explains one credit expert, "is that the penalties do not include jail time. The bad news is that treble damages can be allowed, making the impact potentially very expensive."

A company, for example, that allows customers who complain to avoid paying late fees while collecting from more reticent customers *could* be in violation of the Act. Now, many reading this are probably saying, "True, but how would anyone ever find out?" Before brushing the matter aside, ask yourself how often invoices or billing statements get sent to the wrong customer at your company. Do invoices ever stick together, resulting in one customer getting two invoices? Even if this only happens two or three times a year, there is potential for trouble.

How Effective Are Late Fees?

The CRF asked respondents what percentage of the late fees assessed were actually collected. Over half of those responding indicated that they collected less than half of the amount. Only 19.7% collected more than 75% of their assessments. Two main reasons for charging late fees are:

1. To recoup some of the financial loss associated with the late payment

2. To modify customer behavior

The CRF also asked the respondents if they believed that the threat of a late payment charge helped their companies get paid more promptly. Over half (52.4%) believe the intimidation works.

Should You Implement a Late Fee Policy?

There is no easy answer to this question. Each company has to make this decision for itself. The following is a list of questions to use in evaluating whether a late-fee policy will work at your company:

- If a late-fee policy is put in place, will it be administered uniformly?
- Will the policy generate enough income to make it worth the trouble?

- Will the policy encourage customers to change bad bill-paying habits?

- Do other companies in your industry use late fees? If not, will the introduction of a late-fee policy make your company uncompetitive?

The CRF routinely takes the pulse of the business credit community by doing online surveys. To participate go to www.crfonline.org.

Other Collection Techniques

Collection professionals are an innovate group—they have to be considering the fact that they are trying to get money from businesses that either don't have the money to pay or simply don't want to pay. In addition to all the approaches discussed so far, they generally will try anything that will work and is legal.

TIPS & TECHNIQUES

Collection Tips from the Field: Other

- "Drop the ax" on those customers who do not keep their commitments or provide an acceptable payment plan.

- Align customer service and credit so that problems may be resolved quickly and payment to the company expedited.

- Automate the follow-up scheduling and include *on-screen* contact comments by account.

- Establish monthly meetings with account managers to ask for their assistance in the resolution of collection issues with their accounts.

- Even though it may not be part of their job, encourage the sales force to collect wherever possible.

TIPS & TECHNIQUES CONTINUED

- Generate a list of the ten largest delinquent accounts. Target them for special collection attention.

- Get to know your customers, making it more difficult for them to delay payment to you when they have limited funds and have to decide who to pay today and who not to pay until tomorrow.

- If you are in a low-dollar, high-volume business, consider using summary statements instead of individual invoices for each billing.

- If you are using a lockbox, periodically have a lockbox study completed to ensure that it is in the best possible location.

- Increase contact with the owners or senior managers of known delinquents.

- Increase the frequency of your customer visits. By developing a personal relationship with key customers, you make it more difficult for them to delay payments to you.

- Keep notes of contacts with customers on the network. In that manner, anyone discussing orders can quickly see if there are any outstanding credit issues. This approach allows the collection professional to quote back to the customer who said what and when. It gets the customer's attention and action.

- Meet customers face to face wherever possible. It is more difficult for them to delay payment to someone they know personally.

- Monitor accounts and take action as soon as an account goes past due.

- Offer a small bonus based on results to your collectors.

- Prepare a welcome packet for new customers. Let them know what is expected of them—specifically that they pay you on time.

TIPS & TECHNIQUES CONTINUED

- Put collection stickers on invoices and dunning notices.

- Quickly resolve all disputes and remove the legitimate reasons your customers may have for not paying.

- Redesign your invoice. Make it user friendly and easy for the recipient to figure out how much is owed and when you expect to be paid. Some have had success putting the amount to be paid and the due date in bold letters.

- Send a friendly reminder notice when an invoice goes a few days past due.

- Turn customers who are more than 90 days past due over to a collection agency. The exact point will vary from industry to industry. While turning an account over to a collection agency usually destroys that relationship, remember that the longer you wait, the less likely it is that the account will be collected.

- Use collection stickers from Renton's International Stationery. These are useful in bringing the customers' attention to the fact that payments are past due. Many customers will immediately call and make payment arrangements.

- Visit as many of your customers as possible to help establish that personal relationship.

- Visit late-paying customers personally to inquire about payments.

- Visit the accounts payable Web sites—if companies have them—to determine when your payment will be made. Contact the customer immediately if the payment date is not acceptable.

- Weekly review of the status of the accounts should be made by the chief financial officer (CFO), marketing, and collections department. Those credit and collection professionals

TIPS & TECHNIQUES CONTINUED

who think that CFOs would not be willing to be involved in such a process should note that this recommendation was made by a CFO.

- When dealing with a smaller customer, try to establish a relationship with the owner rather than the accounts payable manager. Then if normal collection techniques don't work, you have an ally in the right corner.

When All Else Fails: Collection Agencies

No matter how competent the collection professional, eventually all will end up with a customer that simply will not pay. When that happens most turn to a collection agency. But, which one? There are so many. The following is a list of guidelines credit and collection professionals can use to help them get the best results from their collection agencies.

- *Use several agencies.* Never depend on just one, no matter how good you believe that agency to be. Many mid-size companies find that using three agencies gives them adequate coverage.

- *Distribute your placements among three agencies and periodically monitor the results.* It's acceptable to give one agency more than its fair share *if* their results warrant a larger piece of the pie.

- *When selecting and evaluating an agency, don't focus entirely on the agency's fees.* Low prices may not translate into the highest return for your company. Evaluate the total dollars returned to your company after the agency's fees. Be wary of fees that are much lower than the rest of the industries. Agencies that offer low fees will sometimes only make a cursory effort to collect leaving the really difficult accounts for someone else.

- *Make sure you understand the agency's fee schedule.* It should be clear and easy to comprehend. If something is not obvious, ask—don't assume. Also, be aware that most agencies' fees are contingent on their collecting something for you. If they are unsuccessful, they earn nothing.

- *Use care in selecting your agencies.* Check references. When checking references, ask:
  - If the reference would use the agency again
  - How long the reference party has been using the agency
  - The party to rate the agency on a scale of one to ten, recognizing that few people will give the very top rating to anyone

- *Make sure the agency is bonded.* This gives you some security in the unlikely event that there is fraud at some point when the agency is handling one of your accounts.

- *Visit the agency periodically unannounced* to see how the day-to-day operations are run.

- *Ask the agency if it is a member of any professional association.* Many belong to The Commercial Law League of America and the best have met the stiff certification standards of that group and carry the desired "certified by the Commercial Law League" designation. To find those agencies, go to www.clla.org.

- *Ask all potential agencies how long they have been in business.* While all new businesses need to start somewhere, your company does not need to be at the head of this line.

- *Turn your accounts over to the agency while there is still a chance of collecting.* Many companies are reluctant to turn accounts over, either for fear of alienating a customer or not wishing to pay the agency fee. When they finally turn the account over, it is no longer collectable. Many companies don't turn over their accounts until they are six months past due. This makes it very difficult for the agency.

- *Approach your agencies for a reduction in fees for all accounts turned over early.* Some agencies will offer a lower rate for those accounts turned over at 60 days.

IN THE REAL WORLD

Good Notes Pay Off

At a recent accounts payable conference, a controller told a story about the toughest credit manager he had ever met. Her name was Vicky, and he was her largest customer. She put his company on credit hold because his company had taken some deductions it was not entitled to. She wanted the money paid before she would release the next order.

Does this story sound familiar? Well, what happened next is unusual. The controller made all sorts of promises and after each one she would reply, "That's what you said last year," or "That's what you said two years ago." She had meticulously documented every conversation they had ever had. He was incredulous. "We were the largest customer and she was putting us on credit hold," he told the group, "and the president of the company backed her up." After that incident, he always made sure that Vicky got paid on time. Vicky knew her stuff, like most credit professionals do, but they don't get the support that Vicky received. Thus, they have to resort to other techniques to ensure that their companies get paid.

- *Don't assume that because one agency can't collect on an account that the account can't be collected.* Some agencies will take accounts that have already been worked by others. Of course, you should expect to pay a higher fee for this service. Since most of these agencies also work on a contingency basis, it costs nothing to place your really bad debts with them.

- *Consider selling uncollectible debts to an investor who buys debt.* You won't get much, but it is better than nothing. Many of these investors sit on the bad debts for a while and then try and collect after the debt has aged—and hopefully the debtor's financial condition has improved. To find one, go to www.debtbuyers.com.

- *Make sure that your collections are held in a separate account from the agency.* Under no circumstances should your funds be commingled with the agency's money.

An Overview of Collection Activities with an International Flair

In a recent survey, 62% of companies admitted to consciously paying their bills late. Add to this number the firms that don't do it on purpose and those who won't admit publicly that they follow such a process, and you'll begin to see why good collection skills and practices are essential to the viability of any company. While the basics of good collection techniques remain the same, effective execution of those strategies is rapidly changing. At a credit conference in London, STA International's Kevin Terrell put some new twists on established techniques that will improve your collection results.

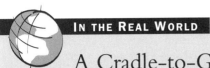

A Cradle-to-Grave Approach to Credit

When Helen Jackson arrived at Proxicom, an Internet consulting firm, she found the same situation as she had at her previous jobs —no formal collections department or procedures. This savvy credit, collections, and billing manager developed an innovative *cradle-to-grave* approach that has made a drastic impact on DSO—a drop of 11 days in one quarter. Jackson says that when she arrived collections were not a high priority. Employees in the finance and marketing departments would make collections calls when they had some free time. Since few people like making these calls, the follow-up got very low priority. When she took over and began calling, she found out that a high percentage of the invoices were incorrect. Since billing and collections were separate, there was no incentive to get the invoices right.

This is where Jackson says the cradle-to-grave concept comes into play. One person is responsible for the account. If there is a billing error, it is fixed by the same individual who would have to make the collection call. Each invoice also contains contact information: A customer who gets an incorrect invoice knows whom to call to get it fixed. Since most customers don't call when there is an error, Jackson makes a courtesy call 15 days after the invoice goes out. She asks if everything is correct and resolves any discrepancies at that point. When she first started calling, customers told her that in the past the company did not call until the payment was 60 days past due.

Needles to say, even when she got the billing corrected, not all customers paid according to terms. However, she did not let that stop her. She would call and the customer's accounts payable clerk generally would tell her that the accounting department dictated that all payments were to be made net 60. She would then call accounting and receive the same story. When she finally got them to get out the contract and review the terms and conditions, they would then pay within the agreed-upon terms.

Jackson says that the finance department understood the cradle-to-grave program and was all for it. However, the outside sales force was not as agreeable. Once they understood that customers liked the fact that they had one person to talk to for all billing-related issues, they were okay with it. She says that getting to know the customers personally helps with the entire cycle.

Collection Policy

The foundation for effective collection tactics is a written collection policy. While many companies have written credit policies, few have formal collection policies. In fact, only a few in the audience raised their hands when Terrell asked who had formalized collection policies. He says that with a written policy there can be no misunderstandings when it comes to collection actions.

Start Date

Many collection pros start their collection calls when an account first goes past due by some given number of days, but Terrell says it is better to call before the due date. He calls this the *customer service* call. It gives the credit manager the opportunity to make sure the invoice has been received, inquire if there are any problems, and remind the customer of the due date.

It is not possible to call every account, and Terrell suggests that the pre–due date calls be focused on those customers who typically pay late. If that's virtually all of your debtors, then focus on the larger accounts. He suggests that these calls be placed to the person responsible for making the payment. The goal is to get a commitment from this individual to make the payment on or before the due date.

Collection Letters

Despite the fact that most people disparage collection letters as an effective tool, many companies still use them. If you do, Terrell offers the following five suggestions:

1. If the letters have not been rewritten for some time, take the time to do so.

2. Create a third-party look for your collection letters. You might establish a *debt recovery* department and have the letters come from that group. If you take this approach, make sure the letters contain a different phone number from the one typically used when calling the credit department.

3. Use two or three letters and keep them short.

4. Change the timing between letters. Otherwise, your customers will quickly notice the pattern and only pay attention to that last letter—the one when you threaten to put them on credit hold.

5. Take care in addressing the letter. It should go to someone high in the debtor's organization—someone who does not typically get collection letters.

Technology

Given recent advances in technology, collectors can now be more effective than ever. Software packages help collection professionals focus on those accounts that need to be called. Imaging, videoconferencing, e-mail, and the Internet are all having a major impact on the efforts of credit and collection professionals today. Those who do not take advantage of these tools will be left in the dust.

The Internet and interactive voice recognition (IVR) systems can also be used to make the most of collectors' limited time. Here's how: A call is made to the IVR unit, and the appropriate passwords and invoice numbers are entered into the phone. Information regarding payment date for each invoice is then given. The collector who verifies upcoming payments in this manner can then focus collection activity on those debtors who have not scheduled payments appropriately.

Similarly, a few companies have put this information on the Internet. By checking the customers' Web site and entering the appropriate passwords and invoice numbers, the collector can determine what payment will be made when and focus the efforts on invoices not scheduled for payment or those scheduled inappropriately.

What You Can Do with E-mail

For starters, Terrell says that e-mail, rather than letters or faxes, should be used for collection efforts. Using document scanning for items such as invoices, proofs of delivery, and other documents that the credit professional might ultimately need to prove a customer has received a shipment. This does not have to be big fancy imaging systems, but rather handheld scanners. Once the documents are imaged they can be attached to an e-mail for easy delivery to the debtor.

But that is not Terrell's most innovative suggestion when it comes to e-mail collections. He suggests that companies purchase a video camera and, rather than a written e-mail, send a video clip of the collection manager asking for payment. The clip is personalized, of course, for the person receiving it. The attachment files for such videos are not overly large, and that will make an impact with your debtors.

In closing, Terrell urged the group to take a day off—not a vacation day as most in attendance hoped—but of their DSO. Credit and collection professionals who incorporate some of Terrell's techniques into their day-to-day collection activities may be able to do just that.

Summary

The success or failure of the collection efforts is typically measured at most companies, the most common benchmark being DSO figures. This will be discussed in great length in Chapter 4.

It is important to remember that very few companies actually collect every dollar they bill. In fact, some professionals believe that if there are no bad debt write-offs, the company has too stringent a credit policy and is not optimizing its sales or profits. This does not mean to imply that credit should be granted to all that show up. However, it does mean that, especially for a company with wide margins, an occasional write-off is not the end of the world.

By following the collection advice discussed in this chapter, collection professionals will be able to collect as much of their firm's money as is humanly possible.

CHAPTER 4

Accounts Receivable Issues

After reading this chapter you will be able to

- Understand the importance of accounts receivable
- Apply cash efficiently and effectively
- Effectively manage the bad debt
- Evaluate the problems that occur when accounts receivable is not updated correctly
- Assess the best accounts receivable techniques

For many companies, the accounts receivable portfolio is its largest asset. Thus, it deserves special care and attention. Effective handling of the portfolio can add to the bottom line, while neglect can cost companies in unseen losses.

Accounts Receivable Strategies to Energize the Bottom Line

Don't be surprised to find the big shots from finance suddenly looking over your shoulder questioning the ways your credit department operates. Accounts receivable has become the darling of those executives desperate to optimize working capital and improve their balance sheet.

Here's a roundup of some of the tactics that have been collected from the best credit managers to squeeze every last cent out of their accounts receivable portfolio:

- Have invoices printed and mailed as quickly as possible. Most customers start the clock ticking when the invoice arrives in their offices. The sooner you can get the invoice to them, the sooner they will pay you. While this strategy will not affect days sales outstanding (DSO), it will improve the bottom line.

- Look for ways to improve invoice accuracy without delaying the mail date.

- Offer more stringent terms where appropriate in your annual credit reviews and with new customers. Consider whether shorter terms might be better for your company.

- Offer financial inducements to customers who agree to pay your invoices electronically.

- If you have not had a lockbox study performed in the last few years, have one done to determine your optimal lockbox location.

- With customers who have a history of paying late, begin your collection efforts before the due date. Call to inquire whether they have the invoice and if everything is in order. Resolve any problems quickly at this point.

- If you have been giving a grace period to those taking discounts after the discount period, reduce or eliminate it.

- Resolve all discrepancies quickly so payment can be made promptly.

- If a customer indicates it has a problem with part of an invoice, authorize partial payments.

- Keep a log of customer problems and analyze it once a month to discover weaknesses in your procedures that cause these quandaries.

- Apply cash the same day the payment is received. Collectors can then spend their time with customers who have not paid rather than annoying ones who have already sent their payment.

- Deal with a bank that makes lockbox information available immediately by fax, or preferably, online. Then when a customer claims it has made a payment, the collector will be able to verify this.

- Look into ways to accept P-cards from customers placing small orders and those who cannot be extended credit on open account terms.

- Benchmark department and individual collectors' performance to pinpoint those areas and individuals in need of additional training.

Review your own policies and procedures to determine if there are any areas that could be tweaked to improve cash flow. Then, when the call comes from executive quarters, you will be ready, and they will be hard pressed to find ways that you fell down on the job.

Dealing with Purchase Orders

Leading credit managers have learned to pay attention to the purchase orders that their companies receive. Specifically, they want to ensure that the purchase order accepted by the salesperson does not include clauses that will ultimately cause trouble for their companies, or even legal difficulties later on. Realistically, the salesperson should have caught the problem, but he or she rarely does. When the customer doesn't pay due to one of these technicalities, it's not the salesperson who will get blamed.

To help avoid a purchase order disaster, credit professionals can take the following steps:

1. *Simply read the purchase order.* Vendors often slip clauses into purchase orders that you would never agree to. One favorite is to include a statement saying the seller will be paid as soon as its customer pays the buyer. This is a risk few companies are willing to tolerate.

2. *Prioritize attachments.* Typically, buyers write purchase orders that contain attachments. These include drawings, specifications, supplementary terms and conditions for work done on company premises, or safety rules for the supplier.

   When including attachments, it is recommended that one of them be a list of priorities to guard against any inconsistencies in the documents. The purchase order should "clearly reference all the attachments, and there should be a recitation as to which attachments are controlling over the others." In the event of any inconsistency between or among these documents, the purchase order shall be controlling over any attachments, and the attachments shall be interpreted using the priority listed.

3. *Take care when reference is made to a buyer's documents in the purchase order.* There are likely to be both helpful and harmful statements in those documents that reference the buyer's material. The buyer may have printed its own terms and conditions on the back of a document. By referring to the document in the purchase order, you may inadvertently refer not only to the price, but also to terms and conditions, which may include warranty disclaimers and limitations of remedies that your company does not intend to give.

   Instead, the recommendation is not to refer to the buyer's documents. Insist that the information is specified in the purchase order. If this is not practical, the following language might work: "Any reference to the purchaser's quotation contained in this purchase order is a reference for convenience only, and no such reference shall be deemed to include any of the purchaser's standard terms and conditions of sale. The seller expressly rejects anything in any of the buyer's documents that is inconsistent with the seller's standard terms and conditions."

Another favorite is to include terms and conditions on the back of the purchase order written in very small print and a pale (almost undecipherable) color.

4. *Be careful of confirming purchase orders.* Often, buyers will place orders via telephone, only to later confirm them with a written purchase order. In oral contracts, the buyer will often want the purchase order to be more than just an offer. Therefore, the buyer will try to show on the purchase order that it is a *confirming purchase order* and cement the oral contract made over the phone. If the buyer does so, the confirming purchase order will satisfy the Uniform Commerical Code (UCC) requirement of a written confirmation unless the other side objects to it within ten days.

More than one cunning purchaser has slipped terms into a confirming purchase order that were nothing like those agreed to orally. Don't fall into the trap of assuming that the confirming purchase order confirms what was actually said on the phone.

Credit professionals who take these few extra steps with regard to purchase orders will limit their troubles.

Quality of Accounts Receivable: Days Sales Outstanding

Many credit professionals are measured on their effectiveness by reviewing the accounts receivable portfolio. The most common measurement is the length of time a sale stays outstanding before being paid. The

Credit Research Foundation (CRF) defines DSO as the average time in days that receivables are outstanding. It helps determine if a change in receivables is due to a change in sales, or to another factor such as a change in selling terms. An analyst might compare the days' sales in receivables with the company's credit terms as an indication of how efficiently the company manages its receivables. Days sales outstanding is occasionally referred to as days receivable outstanding, as well. The formula to calculate DSO is:

$$\frac{\text{Gross Receivables}}{\text{Annual Net Sales} / 365}$$

Quality of Accounts Receivable: Collection Effectiveness Index

Some feel that the quality of the portfolio is dependent to a large extent on the efforts of the collection staff. This is measured by the collection effectiveness index (CEI). The CRF says this percentage expresses the effectiveness of collection efforts over time. The closer to 100% the ratio gets, the more effective the collection effort. It is a measure of the quality of collection of receivables, not of time. Here's the formula to calculate the CEI:

$$\frac{\text{Beginning Receivables} + (\text{Credit Sales}/N) - \text{Ending Total Receivables}}{\text{Beginning Receivables} + (\text{Credit Sales}/N) - \text{Ending Current Receivables}} \times 100$$

N = Number of Months or Days

Quality of Accounts Receivable: Best Possible Days Sales Outstanding

Many credit professionals find fault with using DSO to measure their performance. They feel that a better measure is one based on average terms based on customer payment patterns. The CRF says that this figure expresses the best possible level of receivables. The CRF believes this measure should be used together with DSO. The closer the overall DSO is to the average terms based on customer payment patterns (best possible DSO [BPDSO]), the closer the receivables are to the optimal level. The formula for calculating BPDSO is:

$$\frac{\text{Current Receivables x Number of Days in Period Analyzed}}{\text{Credit Sales for Period Analyzed}}$$

The numbers in the accompanying In The Real World, "National Summary of Domestic Trade Receivables," were supplied by the CRF for use by readers to compare their own performance. In addition to figures for the entire group, the CRF breaks its statistics down by industry —a comparison that is much more meaningful than overall numbers. The CRF performs this survey quarterly and shares the results with all participants. Readers who would like to participate in future surveys can visit the CRF's Web site at www.crfonline.org for details of the latest survey. In addition to the benchmarking DSO survey, from time to time the CRF conducts surveys on other topics of interest to the credit and collection community. Visit the Web site regularly for details on these timely surveys and the CRF's thrice yearly conferences.

Bad-Debt Reserves

Inevitably, no matter how good the credit professional, a company will have a customer that does not pay its debts. Most companies understand that bad debts are simply part of doing business and reserve for bad debts. In fact, many believe that a company with no bad debts is not doing a good job. The reason being that if the company loosened its credit terms slightly, the company would greatly increase its sales and, even after accounting for the bad debts, its profits. Thus, most companies plan

IN THE REAL WORLD

National Summary of Domestic Trade Receivables

for Quarter Ending September 30, 2001

Industry Group (Standard Industry Classification Code)	CEI	DSO	BPDSO	% Current	% over 90 Days
Total—This Quarter	76.62	44.70	32.40	77.60	1.35
Total—Last Quarter	77.80	44.70	32.30	78.57	1.62
Total—Year Ago	80.15	43.20	32.80	81.27	1.40
Apparel and Other Finished Products (2300)	85.30	55.91	37.47	81.97	0.29
Business Services (7300)	66.23	49.40	30.60	63.38	6.21
Chemicals and Allied Products (2800)	82.00	44.00	34.66	84.40	0.76
Electronic and Electronic Equipment (3600)	71.35	51.55	34.90	71.01	1.95
Fabricated Metal Products (3400)	77.55	42.75	34.85	78.03	2.00
Food and Kindred Products (2000)	87.60	23.10	19.77	87.80	0.57
Industrial and Commercial Machinery (3500)	70.50	53.02	31.80	69.56	2.70
Measuring and Analyzing Instruments (3800)	72.05	50.10	35.35	69.79	3.40
Miscellaneous Manufacturing Industries (3900)	77.42	44.10	39.90	78.75	0.15
Paper and Allied Products (2600)	87.71	33.20	29.45	86.61	0.35
Primary Metal Industries (3300)	75.40	43.50	30.45	73.51	3.50
Printing, Publishing, and Allied Industries (2700)	73.72	47.40	32.50	69.64	4.45

Stone Clay and Concrete					
Products (3200)	74.69	41.86	31.10	82.04	3.94
Wholesale Trade—					
Durable Goods (5000)	72.35	44.75	30.37	73.01	2.22
Wholesale Trade—					
Nondurable Goods (5100)	74.65	45.63	36.50	79.83	1.00

for bad debt, monitor it, and periodically, depending on the company's outlook, revise projections and credit policy to allow for an increase or decrease.

For example, as the economy goes into a recession, most companies will experience an increase in bad debts if their credit policy remains static. So, in light of declining economic conditions, companies should either increase their bad-debt reserves or tighten the credit policy. Similarly, if the economy is improving, a company would take reverse actions, either decreasing the reserve for bad debts or loosening the credit policy.

Many companies take advantage of a favorable economy to expand their customer base. They might simultaneously increase the bad-debt reserve and loosen credit policy. Obviously, these decisions are typically made at a fairly high level. Other factors will also come into play in establishing a bad-debt reserve. Industry conditions are key and can often be quite different than the state of the economy. This is especially true when competition comes from foreign markets.

There is no one set way to calculate the reserve for bad debts. Many simply take a percentage of sales or outstanding accounts receivable, or they make some other relatively uncomplicated calculation.

IN THE REAL WORLD

An Alternative Formula to Calculate a Reserve for Bad Debt

"Frankly, I would avoid such methodologies," says one seasoned credit pro. Having put in 15 years at the director or higher level doing commercial credit, this pro suggests doing more work at the beginning to get more reliable figures. The following are his recommendations:

1. Calculate a line-by-line reserve, which includes accounts comprising 80% of your accounts receivable balance, indicating likely amount uncollectable for each. You might include your largest 100 accounts, for example.

2. Do a similar line-by-line analysis for those accounts with significant past-due balances (you can use a cutoff, such as only accounts with $X over X days past due). Be sure not to duplicate your effort in 1 above.

3. For the remaining accounts, use your historical bad-debt percentage and apply it to the remaining total accounts receivable. This would include, for example, all non–past-due, non–top-100 accounts receivable. Take that dollar amount, and multiply by your historical bad-debt percentage.

4. Add the sums of 1, 2, and 3 to get your required reserve amount.

This professional cautions credit managers against taking the "lazy" way of trying to manage your portfolio from too high a level. He says that his method has worked for portfolios ranging in size from $2 million to $500 million in accounts receivable and is "above and beyond the call of duty" (read: defensible) according to most auditors. Credit professionals charged with setting up a bad-debt reserve might find this approach produces better numbers than the simpler ones sometimes used.

How to Reduce Your Bad-Debt Write-Offs

Most credit and collection professionals would love to be able to brag about having no bad-debt write-offs. Few can. While a goal of reducing the amount of bad debt write-offs to zero might be unrealistic in most industries, keeping that number as low as possible is something within the control of today's credit managers. The following seven techniques will help you keep your numbers as low as possible:

1. *Call early.* Don't wait until the account goes 30 or even 60 days past due before calling customers about late payments. Such delays can mean that, in the case of a financially unstable company, a second and perhaps even a third shipment will be made to a customer who ultimately will pay for naught. Some professionals even call a few days before the payment is due to ensure that everything is in order and the customer has everything it needs to make a timely payment. By beginning your calling campaign as early as possible, it is possible to uncover shaky situations. Even if payment is not received for the first delivery, future orders are not accepted, effectively reducing bad-debt write-offs.

2. *Communicate, communicate, communicate.* Keep the dialogue open with everyone involved. This not only includes your customers, but the sales force as well. In many cases, they are in a better position than the credit manager to know when a customer is on thin ice. With good lines of communication between sales and credit, it is possible to avoid taking some of those orders that will ultimately have to be written off.

3. *Follow up, follow up, follow up.* Continual follow up with customers is important, whether you're trying to collect on a timely basis or attempting to avoid a bad-debt write-off. If the customer knows you will call every few days or will be calling to track the

status of promises made, it is much more likely to pay. This can also be the case of the squeaky wheel getting the grease, or in this case the money, when cash is tight.

4. *Systematize.* Many collection professionals keep track of promises and deadlines by hand, on a pad or calendar. Items tend to fall through the cracks with this approach. Invest some money either in prepackaged software or in developing your own in-house, and the likelihood of losing track of customers diminishes. Some accounting programs have a tracking capability that many have not taken the time to learn. If your software has such a facility, use it.

5. *Specialize.* Set up a group of one or more individuals who do nothing but try to collect receivables that are overdue. By having experts on staff to handle such work, you will improve your collection rate and speed.

6. *Credit hold.* Putting customers on credit hold early in the picture will sometimes entice a payment from someone who really had no intention of paying you. This technique is particularly effective with customers who rely heavily on your product and would be hard put to get it elsewhere. Of course, if you sell something that many other vendors sell as well, putting a potentially good customer on hold could backfire.

7. *Small claims court.* Some credit professionals have had great success in collecting smaller amounts by taking the customer to small claims court. The limits for such actions vary by state but can be as high as $10,000.

While these techniques will not necessarily squeeze money from a bankrupt client, they will help you get as much as possible as soon as possible from as many of your customers as possible. This can be especially

Getting Accounts Receivable Aging under Control

Reducing outstanding receivables was high on H. Bruce Watson's list of priorities when he discovered that 27% of the outstanding accounts receivable portfolio of one of the divisions of Air Products and Chemical Inc. was more than 90 days past due. This manager of retail credit services knew what to do. In 1993, he says, one division was split off from the parent company. However, the accounts receivable and accounting functions stayed with the parent. No one was assigned specific responsibility for the receivables or following up on the collections. In fact, the biggest reason the receivables got so old was that no one was contacting the customers when a payment became past due. All indications were that the problem would get worse if left unattended. Watson had a meeting with the top manager in that organization. That manager gave his approval to attack the problem. He gave Watson carte blanche to do whatever he had to do to get the problem under control.

Watson set up a time line for handling the accounts. When an account became more than 60 days past due, sales was notified. In the period from 60 to 90 days past due, sales would pursue the account in whatever manner it saw best. However, after the 90th day, the account was turned back over to his department for handling as he saw fit. Sales would have no say in what was done after that unless this general manager signed off on the stoppage. This is where most collection efforts bog down—when senior management interferes at the behest of sales. But not in this case.

Watson explains that this manager made where he stood on this issue quite clear. In a meeting with members of the sales force to discuss this issue, he told them he was going to write his phone number on the blackboard so they could write it down and call him whenever they had a problem. Then he took a piece of chalk and drew a line across the board—no numbers. Sales got the message.

important in avoiding preference actions with clients who eventually do file. The quicker you get the clock ticking, the more likely you are to be able to avoid preference claims.

Electronic Payments/Automated Clearinghouse

One of the ways to improve DSO and reduce collection costs is to receive payments electronically. Traditionally, this was done through wire transfers and was only used for large dollar collections or from customers of questionable credit history (for payment in advance) as wire transfers are costly.

However, there is another alternative that has been gaining favor. These are payments through the automated clearinghouse (ACH)—a mechanism most frequently associated with consumer transactions. The most common types of payments made through this mechanism are direct deposit of payroll and Social Security payments. These are examples of ACH credits.

Some readers may have their mortgage payments or life insurance premiums automatically deducted from their bank accounts. These are examples of ACH debits.

As companies look for ways to conduct business electronically, the low cost and ease of the ACH made it an ideal mechanism for those looking to pay their bills electronically. The National Automated Clearinghouse Association, now called the Electronic Payment Association, is a treasure house of information for those looking to increase their knowledge in this arena (see www.nacha.org).

As companies adopt some of the electronic billing products discussed in Chapter 2, they will begin to see the advantages of electronic payments and begin to look at the ACH more favorably for business-to-business payments.

Electronic Payments: Background

As most reading this are well aware, check fraud is an enormous problem in the United States, but not in other countries. The reason for this is simple—the rest of the world does not rely on checks the way the United States does. In fact, most companies and individuals in Europe write few, if any, checks in a given year. For the rest of the world, electronic payments are the standard way of doing business. Individuals are accustomed to having their bank accounts debited for utility bills, phone bills, and so on.

Automated Clearinghouse Credits and Debits

The Association for Financial Professionals (formerly the Treasury Management Association) offers the following definitions:

- *Automated clearinghouse credits* are originated by the payor to move funds from the payor's account to the receiver's (payee's) account. Automated clearinghouse credits must be preauthorized, though not necessarily in writing.

- *Automated clearinghouse debits* are originated by the payee to draw funds out of the receiver's account and deposit them

IN THE REAL WORLD

Implementing an Automated Clearinghouse Debit Program

Core-Mark International, a food and tobacco distributor/broker, has customers of all sizes. This makes collecting a challenge. However, its regional credit manager, Douglas Marx, is up to the job. He is successfully implementing an ACH debit program for his company and, in a short period of time, has convinced more than 140 customers to participate. The time and expense associated with collecting prompted Core-Mark to initiate its electronic funds transfer (EFT) program. This was especially true with regard to some of the smaller customers, the number of which was huge in comparison with the amount of time available.

In many instances, the sales force was responsible for collecting from customers. When a customer has multiple locations, the salespeople can end up chasing all over town. Their time is better spent on other matters. Getting sales to cooperate in any collection initiative can be a challenge. Marx's main tool with the sales group was education. Once they understood how the program works, and saw how it would make their lives a little easier, they were willing to work with customers. The salesperson now gives a new customer an EFT form when he gives them a credit application.

Selecting customers for the program initially required some finesse. Each month he would review sales and target those companies with multiple locations. He realized that not every customer will be amenable to the program, so he avoided those who are not accustomed to new technology. He spends his time where he thinks he has the best chances of success. In the past, it was always Core-Mark pushing the program, but recently the company has had a few requests from customers interested in participating.

The complaints have been minimal. In general, customers don't like it when they don't know when the money is coming out of their account. This is a complaint that many have about ACH programs.

into the payee's account. Debits must be preauthorized in writing by the receiver.

Cash Discounts and Days Sales Outstanding

Do you believe cash discounts are effective in encouraging customers to pay early, thus reducing DSO? The CRF wondered also and recently conducted a study to determine the answer. The results are shared here. As you will see, the study was well worth doing, and the outcomes are not always what credit professionals might expect.

Background

Cash discounts are widely regarded as an inducement to get the buyer to pay before the maturity date on the invoice. Discounts offered can vary by industry, season, size of order, past payment performance, and a variety of other issues.

The formula used to determine whether a company should take the discount or not is:

$$(\text{Discount rate} \times 360)/\text{number of days saved}$$

So, in the 2/10 net 30 example, the rate at which a company would be indifferent to whether the discount is taken or not is $(.02 \times 360)/20$, or 36% per annum. Thus, a company should take the discount any time its cost of capital is under 36%, or virtually always unless rampant inflation pushes interest rates above that level.

Survey Results

Well over half (57.7%) of the companies participating in the survey offered discounts to their customers to induce early payment. Few companies (18.6%) reevaluate their discount offered as their cost of money changes. However, over one-third (35.9%) do reevaluate the discount offered as market conditions change. Thus, a company that didn't offer a discount might consider offering one if a new aggressive competitor appeared or to induce large year-end sales. Most companies (76.9%) allow their customers a grace period averaging 6.5 days (median figure: five days).

When companies offer an early payment discount, they do not necessarily offer it to every customer. In fact, many don't, according to the survey:

- 38.3% offer early-payment discounts to fewer than one quarter of their customers

- 3.3% offer the discounts to between one quarter and one half of their customers
- 7.2% offer the discounts to between one half and three quarters of their customers
- 51.1% offer the discount to more than three quarters of their customers

Amazingly, when offered the cash discount, not all customers take it. In fact the survey showed that:

- 26.4% report that less than one quarter of their customers took the discount
- 17.5% report that between one quarter and one half of their customers took the discount
- 14.2% say that between one half and three quarters take the discount
- 43.1% indicate that more than 75% took the early-payment discount

Determining the Cutoff Date

Much debate goes on between customers and suppliers about when the payment was actually received and whether the customer really qualified for the early-payment discount. The survey asked the respondents how they quantified this decision. Here's what the credit professionals responding to the survey indicated:

- Date of check (4.9%)
- Postmark date on the envelope (25.2%)
- Date of receipt of check at lockbox (30.5%)
- Date of receipt of check at the accounts receivable processing center (6.9%)
- Date of electronic data interchange transmission (6.9%)

- Date prearranged with customer (2.0%)
- Other (2.0%)

Collecting Unearned Discounts

Customers who take the early-payment discount when paying on time can be truly frustrating to the credit community—and there are tons that take this approach. Almost 90% of those responding to the CRF survey indicated that they charge back for the unearned discount. However, collecting the discount is another story. When asked how aggressively the discounts were pursued, with 1 being very aggressive and 5 being low priority, here's what the group had to say:

$$1 = 20.5\%$$
$$2 = 17.6\%$$
$$3 = 24.2\%$$
$$4 = 13.7\%$$
$$5 = 24.2\%$$

But, are they successful? On average, 52.37% of the unearned discounts is eventually collected. Several spectacularly successful collection professionals bias this number, since the median response to this question came in at a flat 50%.

Effect on Days Sales Outstanding

The final question, and the real purpose of the survey, was to determine if offering an early-payment discount had a positive effect on DSO. Two-thirds of the group believed early-payment discounts improve DSO results, 15.2% don't think so, and 17.2% don't know.

Most credit professionals have not measured the impact of the cash discount on DSO. However, for the 19.4% who did, the following is a breakdown of the impact:

- One to five days (52.6%)
- Six to ten days (23.7%)
- 11 to 15 days (13.2%)
- 16 to 20 days (10.5%)

Summary

For many companies, the accounts receivable portfolio is its largest asset. Proper care and treatment of this jewel falls under the credit umbrella. When the job is done correctly, additional benefits fall to the bottom line. Thus, it is a responsibility not to be taken lightly.

CHAPTER 5

Handling Deduction Issues

After reading this chapter you will be able to

- Evaluate the unearned discounts and unauthorized deduction problem at your company
- Work with customers to eliminate the discount/deduction problems
- Work internally to minimize the problem
- Recommend techniques that will keep the problem at bay

Not only do credit and collection professionals have to worry about collecting their company's money, they also have to be concerned about collecting all of it. The two largest causes for short payment —and credit professionals' migraines—are unearned discounts and unauthorized deductions.

What Is an Unearned Discount?

Many companies offer a small discount for those customers who pay their invoices early. Typically, a company selling on open account will offer 2/10 net 30. This gives customers the right to pay the full invoice amount 30 days after receiving the goods. However, if the payment is made after ten days, the customer can pay 98% of the invoice, thus saving 2%. While this may not seem like a big deal, it adds up and works out to a rate of return in excess of 36%.

The problem occurs, over and over again, when the customer takes the discount and then doesn't pay within the discount period. Now, if we were only talking about a few extra days, most companies would probably ignore the issue. However, unfortunately, a few extra days is rarely the problem. Many customers take the discount and pay at 30 or 35 or 45 days—or even longer.

What Is an Unauthorized Deduction?

Unearned deductions cause even more headaches for credit and collection professionals than unearned discounts. At least with the discount issue it is fairly easy to calculate and analyze the problem. Unauthorized deductions are reductions customers make on their invoices for any one of dozens of valid or invalid reasons, including:

- Short shipment
- Damaged goods
- Missing documentation
- Not following retailers shipping instructions
- Freight charges
- Insurances charges
- Advertising allowances
- Rebates

Why Have Unauthorized Deductions Become Such an Issue?

The best customers send along the remittance advice that explains what the deductions are for. However, many accounting systems do not have the capabilities to provide adequate detail or the customers don't see the necessity of sending along the backup information. When the accounts receivable manager receives the payment, he or she then has to apply the payment. Since the payment doesn't match any of the outstanding invoices, the accounts receivable professional then has a problem applying cash.

Selling to Retailers

While unauthorized deductions have become a problem for most manufacturers, those selling to retailers appear to be hit the hardest. The problem has gotten so bad that there have been several newspaper articles

IN THE REAL WORLD

Outsourcing Deduction Management Companies

Credit professionals looking for help dealing with their deduction problems can contact one of the three organizations listed below. All work to collect unauthorized deductions and unearned discounts for their clients. The companies are:

1 Pyramid Group: 513-791-5535; www.pyramidgroup.com

2 Internal Audit Bureau: 717-689-0590; www.iabinc.com

3 Creditek: 201-952-0404; www.credditek.com

Additionally, there is some software on the market that helps credit and collection professionals deal with deductions. It should be noted that this software is not inexpensive.

Software

- GETPAID 800-395-9996; www.getpaid.com

- I-many Deduction Management System 800-949-1229; www.imany.com

in publications such as the *Wall Street Journal* and the *New York Times* about the extent of the problem. We should be clear to point out that not all retailers fall into the unreasonable category when it comes to taking unauthorized deductions. Needless to say, the sources in most of the articles are anonymous. However, they came from enough different sources for the newspapers to give credence to the stories. Some of the demands being made by a few retailers are:

- Sellers were asked to give cash back to the retailer or make other concessions to improve the retailers' bottom line.

- Payments were delayed with no notice being given to the supplier.

- Sellers were asked to give back money because their products did not produce the anticipated sales.

TIPS & TECHNIQUES

Ways to Eliminate Deduction Problems

- Ignore the first offense, send a warning with the second, and after that, bill back amounts and handle as any other invoice.

- Implement improved procedures for customer returns and make sure all customers are aware of both the new and existing procedures for returns.

- Personally visit the worst abusers to determine if there are any problems that should be resolved on your end. If not, make it clear that the unauthorized deductions and unearned discounts will not be allowed.

Dealing with the Deduction Problem

What follows on the next few pages are quick tips from real life credit and collection professionals. These suggestions came from various surveys taken by *IOMA's Report on Managing Credit Receivables and Collections* from those who have implemented them in their day-to-day operations. Many can easily be included in the day-to-day operations of the credit department and will help ameliorate the problem.

Eliminate the Problem

In the best of all worlds, unauthorized deductions would be eliminated. While few credit and collection professionals have managed to achieve that goal, by aiming at it, some have come close. When a customer realizes that the credit and collection staff of its vendor is not going to allow it to take deductions without good cause, the number of deductions is likely to decrease with the customer only taking those that it feels it has a reasonable chance of being accepted.

 TIPS & TECHNIQUES

General Tips

- Communicate your requirements to customers. To make this strategy truly effective, sales must be involved in the discussion.

- Implement a credit memo policy. Use stickers on invoices asking customers to call instead of just taking a deduction, which may be unauthorized.

- Put deductions into system for follow-up calls as with any other late payment.

- Use a third-party collection firm to collect these funds on your behalf.

General Deduction Advice

The advice regarding the handling of customers who take unauthorized deductions and unearned discounts willy nilly is broken into several categories. Some of the suggestions, however, are more generalized and as such, are grouped together in the accompanying tips and techniques table.

Preventing Unauthorized Deductions

Of course, the best way to get rid of unwanted deductions is to prevent them from occurring in the first place. While it may not seem possible

TIPS & TECHNIQUES

Ways to Prevent Deduction Problems

- Educate the sales force to resolve problems before the invoice is paid.

- If deductions or discounts are not collected, amounts are deducted from broker and sales budget.

- Make customers aware that unauthorized deductions and unearned discounts will not be allowed. When they realize you mean business, a good portion will stop taking them.

- The first time an unearned discount is taken, send a letter explaining the problem. Include a statement advising that if future unauthorized or unearned discounts are taken, the entire discount program will be placed in jeopardy.

- To avoid unauthorized deductions, verify that the purchase order matches your terms of sale. If it does not, send it back to the customer for corrections.

- When starting a policy of disallowing unearned discounts, call or send a letter. Leave the dollar amount of the discount outstanding.

to the uninitiated, as you will see from the advice included in Tips & Techniques "Ways to Prevent Deduction Problems," there are techniques that can be used to prevent the customer from taking deductions it is not entitled to.

TIPS & TECHNIQUES

Ways to Resolve Deduction Problems

- As soon as a deduction is made, determine whether the deduction is valid. If not, immediately send the customer a fax requesting reimbursement.

- Determine if there is one root cause for a large portion of deductions. When the reason is identified, it is possible to resolve the issue.

- Immediately phone the contact to resolve the dispute. If the first contact person refuses to resolve the matter, move up the ladder. Most who use this strategy report that going over the head of the recalcitrant contact changes the mood, and the contact becomes more cooperative on future encounters.

- Send a follow-up letter and form showing the dollar amount disallowed, the date of the check, along with a copy of the postmark on the envelope for each amount. Most customers will pay on receiving such documentation and stop taking unearned discounts in the future.

- Set up a customer-complaint system. Customers can call the customer service department with their complaint. An online complaint can be e-mailed to the responsible department and handled immediately to the satisfaction of both parties. Credits can be issued, where appropriate, before the deduction is taken.

Resolving Deduction Issues

Many credit and collection professionals learn the hard way that some deduction issues are actually the fault of their own company—yes it does occasionally happen. When this occurs, the effective credit professional gets involved and resolves the issue. Even if it isn't your company, it may be imperative that the credit professional get involved to get the matter resolved.

Strategies

Rather than take the quick tip approach, some professionals will prefer to take a more thorough strategy. Some strategies that have worked for others in the field are:

- *Rebill the customer immediately for the deduction.* Include a copy of the group service agreement outlining the deduction policy with a request for payment within 15 days. If payment is not received, inform the customer that the agreement will be canceled. This approach requires backing from senior management.

- *When a new account is set up, send a letter introducing the credit manager along with a copy of the policies and procedures.* To establish a more personal relationship with the customer's accounts payable manager, follow up with a phone call.

- *Resolve complaints and discrepancies quickly.* The sooner the issues are resolved, the faster the deductions will disappear, and the customer will learn that you will not tolerate unauthorized deductions.

- *As soon as the deduction is identified, call the customer and request the backup paperwork.* If it is provided, research it immediately, and get back to the customer. If it is not furnished, continue to call the customer to request the information. If all else fails, have the salesperson request the backup data.

- *If the volume of unauthorized deductions is high, assign one staff member to chase down and collect this money.*

- *Within 48 hours of receiving a payment with an unauthorized deduction, advise the customer of the disallowed deduction and request immediate payment of the amount not approved.*

- *Implement the 80/20 rule.* Reorganize the department so that one person handles the worst offenders. One credit manager reports that seven of his customers represent 75% of the unauthorized deductions. He assigned one staff member to handle the deductions on those seven accounts.

- *Empower the billing staff to review and follow-up on short-paid invoices to free the collections staff to pursue larger collection problems.* Train the billing staff on proper procedures, including running reports, setting up standard form letters, and documenting internal systems.

- *Those who offer nonstandard terms often find that their customers calculate discounts incorrectly.* Prepare a standard memo thanking the customer for the prompt payment. Then inform the customer that the discount was calculated incorrectly, and show the correct calculation. Not only does this approach bring in the money for the credit professional who uses it, but she says it also reduces the number of phone calls into the credit department.

- *Work closely with the sales department.* When customers take unauthorized deductions, force the credit department to work with sales to resolve the problems. The accounting manager who takes this approach reports double benefits: Her receivables aging improved, and the credit department enhanced its relationship with the sales force.

- *Visit recalcitrant customers to explain the company's policies regarding unauthorized deductions.* This tactic works best if the company has a clear deduction policy to share with the customer.

- *Outsource the function to a third-party deduction management firm that specializes in this service.*

- *Analyze and eliminate the root causes of your deduction problems.*

IN THE REAL WORLD

Credit Pro Guns Down Unauthorized Deductions

When Remington Arms Company hired credit manager Vicki C. Sharp, unauthorized deductions were a serious problem especially by the big chain stores that demand total adherence to their rules. Through a variety of techniques, she effectively eliminated 90% of the problem. The unauthorized deductions were averaging 150 days past due and were out of hand. The function was handled in Delaware and the people at that location knew they were losing their jobs. Whether it was the knowledge of their impending job loss or that they lacked the expertise to handle the job is not clear. They simply had no incentive to resolve the deductions.

Sharp says she started from scratch, bringing the operation to North Carolina. She hired new people and trained them. The number of claims that had not been researched was high. The company also brought in temporary workers to try to get the workload under control. They even brought in a third-party firm that specializes in collection of unauthorized deductions for about six months.

However, the company's long-term goal was to have their own people handle the work.

Sharp does not intend to let the problem get out of hand again. She says the best defense is to be a good detective and do it the way the chain stores demand. This means that as soon as she receives a check with a deduction, she goes into action. The item is immediately researched and a determination is made to see if the company complied with the customer's guidelines. If Remington is in the right, she immediately drafts a denial letter and backs it up with all the documentation. This includes a copy of the customer's check. This gives them everything they need. With this approach, Remington generally gets 90% of its claims paid back.

Occasionally, even after providing all this documentation, the customer still does not repay the deduction. If the dollars warrant it, Sharp visits the customer, bringing along all the unpaid claims with the documentation. She sits and visits with them and reviews the material. Typically, she only has to do this once and then has a friend for life. Afterward, if she has another problem with that company, she always calls the person she visited with—even if they no longer have responsibility for the deductions.

She recommends that credit professionals be good and timely detectives. Research the deduction immediately and get rid of it. If another department is responsible, work with that department. When dealing with the chains, this can mean getting shipping to move a label from the right side of the box to the left. She says that occasionally other departments cannot change the way they are handling the issue. Then she sits down with the chain and tries to negotiate with the chain over the issue. Sometimes she gets a deviation and sometimes she doesn't—but she always tries.

Many reading these suggestions will think that they involve too much effort given the amount of the deduction. On one level, they are correct. However, the goal is not only to collect money for the unauthorized deduction, but to change customers' behavior. If they know you will chase the money, they may stop taking the deductions After all, the customer must do a lot of work as well.

Summary

Deductions are a serious dilemma for the credit and collection professional. The problem shows no signs of abating. The best one can probably hope for is to try and keep the issue under control. This requires constant and steady effort and attention. Without that, the problem will mushroom, taking all a company's profits with it.

CHAPTER 6

Interacting with Sales and Marketing

After reading this chapter you will be able to

- Understand the importance of the sales–credit relationship
- Develop a good working relationship with the sales department
- Recognize what credit can do to make sales job a little easier
- Make a pitch for credit at sales meetings

At some companies, the sales group calls the credit department "the sales prevention department." The horrendous part of this scenario is not that sales is name calling, but that credit is not perceived as doing anything to boost sales. Although the next statement is not likely to win friends in the credit community, I'm going to make it anyway. It is credit's job to support the sales group and do whatever it can to find ways to make a sale happen. This does not mean rolling over and agreeing to every sale proposed. It does mean finding ways to work with the sales department to make the sale happen, that is, suggesting a letter of credit, alternative terms, and so on.

Importance of Establishing a Good Relationship with Sales

When sales and credit are at each other's throat, everyone loses. Much time and effort is wasted trying to thwart each other rather than growing sales. If a good relationship is established, then sales is less likely to try and go over the credit professional's head on those rare occasions when there is no way to approve a credit. In those organizations where sales and credit get along, sales are likely to increase, sales is likely to provide credit with information it needs but might not come across in its own investigations, and credit provides leads to sales that it might not have gotten through its normal channels. Everyone wins.

There are even more important reasons for credit to get along with sales. For starters, if it ever comes down to a choice between a good salesperson and a good credit person, nine out of ten companies will keep the salesperson. Additionally, as some companies move to establish a financial customer service department (the combination of the order entry, credit, and customer service functions), some are putting the responsibility under marketing. Should this occur in your organization, it is far better to have a good relationship with the people who run the sales and marketing functions than to be known as that troublemaker who always prevents their sales and thus their commissions. Credit managers who have this reputation with their sales managers should not be surprised to find themselves out on the street at their new boss's first opportunity after credit is moved under marketing. It's simply a matter of self-preservation. The moral of this story is get along with sales.

Dealing with Being Overruled

When a sales-credit encounter happens, as it does every day, credit professionals should keep track of the activity. Why? The reason is that the credit professional should not be blamed when the account in question goes bad.

Sales–Credit Encounter

The following scenario happens more frequently than credit professionals would like to admit. A salesperson brings in a big sale from a questionable customer. Often, especially if the salesperson really knows the customer is unacceptable, the order will show up in the credit department late on a Friday afternoon marked *Rush,* or it will come at the end of a month or quarter or some other reporting period. When the credit professional reviews the order and the customer's financial data, he realizes that the customer does not meet standards and turns the order down.

Now here comes the ugly part. The salesperson is not willing to see the commission go down the drain, so he simply goes over the credit manager's head. Unfortunately, salespeople are usually persuasive about making their case and frequently get the credit manager's decision overturned. Of course, such action on the part of management completely undermines the credit manager's authority and credibility, and the next time the same situation arises, the salesperson is only too happy to repeat the same action.

Without documentation, it is likely that no one will remember that the credit manager did not want to make the sale. Even if the salesperson remembers, he is not going to mention it if the debt can't be collected.

Even with the documentation, the credit professional must proceed carefully. No one likes to be reminded of poor decisions. Thus, the credit professional who wants to move upward has to be careful of how this information is relayed to management. "I told you so" is generally not a good course of action.

A few companies make the salesperson responsible for collections of their own bad accounts or deduct commissions for bad sales. However, these companies are few and far between.

Credit's Role: To Make the Sale Happen

So exactly what is credit's role within the organization? Ask most credit professionals this question and they will tell you it is to protect the company's accounts receivable portfolio and prevent sales to bad risk customers. This is not correct. The credit manager's role is to limit risk while finding ways to make sales happen. The credit manager must be creative and innovative in doing this for, as most reading this are well aware, sales will often find the most noncreditworthy customers.

One of the other benefits of looking for ways to make sales happen is that often in doing this the credit professional will uncover those few fraudulent situations where the potential customer is a crook looking to take the company for a ride. In the process of the normal credit investigation, the credit manager may uncover a fictitious address, phony references, and so on. This is the type of sale the credit manager wants to prevent—and the sales manager will be thankful that it was stopped.

There is one piece of advice in these circumstances that some credit professionals sometimes forget. Be gracious if you uncover such a situation. Don't rub it in. The salesperson will feel bad enough about having been taken by the con artist and is likely to listen to the credit professional in the future—as long as he is not constantly reminded of his mistake. It may be hard, especially when dealing with an obnoxious salesperson. However, bite your tongue every time you have the impulse to mention the unfortunate incident even if it means, as one credit professional aptly says, biting a hole right through your tongue.

Maintaining the Sales–Credit Relationship

Given the fact that the natural focus of the sales department's responsibilities often puts it in direct conflict with credit, maintaining a decent relationship takes effort—effort that is unlikely to be put forth by the sales staff. Thus, it falls on the shoulders of the credit professional to

TIPS & TECHNIQUES

Maintaining the Relationship

- Attend the annual sales meetings, and make it your business to get to know the salespeople who give you the hardest time.

- Communicate regularly with the sales staff so they are aware of the credit policy and the company's expectations from its customers.

- Communicate the good news about customers as well as the bad.

- Discuss the customer or transaction with sales from a business perspective rather than from either the sales or credit perspective.

- Have a monthly meeting with the salespeople. When they begin to understand that their customers are not paying or are paying very late, they will be more receptive to complying with a good credit policy.

- Hold quarterly meetings with the sales department to discuss progress on open unresolved issues.

- Involve sales in the effort to gather information on the financial stability of current customers.

- Keep the sales staff informed whenever an account is put on credit hold. Make sure the salesperson hears it from the credit department and not from an outraged customer.

- Make joint customer visits with the sales force. This reinforces to the customer that sales and credit are on the same team and cannot be played off against each other. It also reduces the likelihood that the salesperson will tell the customer, behind the credit manager's back, that it is acceptable to pay 30 days late.

- Make the credit department staff more available to sales. Returning calls promptly and actually visiting local sales offices will accomplish this communications goal. Make it a point to visit local sales offices whenever you are out of town either on a customer visit or attending an industry credit meeting.

- Meet monthly or quarterly with the sales director to explain credit lines on the account. In time, he or she will begin to understand why certain accounts are held to their limits while others can be increased.

- Occasionally, go out to lunch with the salesperson. Obviously, this will only work if the sales force is small.

- Update the sales staff in writing about matters that are of mutual interest.

- Whenever possible, rather than reject an order, try to find a way to meet the salesperson halfway by suggesting alternative credit terms or offering a lower limit.

- Be the bearer of good news as well as bad. If, while doing annual reviews, you find that certain customers will have their credit limits increased, notify the appropriate salesperson immediately. This is one way to lose the sales prevention department moniker.

- Expand the focus of the department to include both credit and financial service. This does not mean lowering credit standards, but rather encompassing the customer service aspect of the transaction. A number of companies are revamping and reengineering the credit and customer service functions into one group called customer financial services.

- If you find it necessary to put a customer on credit hold, give the sales department the courtesy of informing them of this fact before they try to enter a new order. A side benefit of this approach is that they may actually collect the payment in an attempt to avoid having a prized customer (that is, large) put on credit hold.

- Improve communication between sales staff and finance department through electronic online information access. Implement through use of laptops connecting to database-specific information.

- Meet on a regular basis with sales. Issues such as financial capability and market potential expectations can be discussed. This approach creates a unified perspective of how the company as a whole should set priorities.

- Set up regular meetings with sales to air any concerns and ongoing problems.

- Use a faster routing mechanism, for example, Lotus, for faster customer credit decisions.

- Visit customers with the salesperson responsible for the account. Discuss it beforehand and explain any problems you may have. If necessary, you can play good cop/bad cop with the credit professional, inevitably, getting the part of the bad cop.

- When it becomes necessary to place a customer on credit hold, notify the salesperson responsible for the account before he or she writes more orders. If the reason for the hold is past-due payments, the salesperson may expedite the collection in order to get another order pushed through.

work at keeping the relationship on course. Tips & Techniques, "Maintaining the Relationship," provides some tips that credit professionals can use to keep the relationship on an even keel. The tips, as do the remainder in this chapter, come from real-life credit professionals who are sharing the tactics that have worked for them. Readers who incorporate some of their peers' advice into their own routines are likely to find a smoother ongoing day-to-day interaction with sales.

Improving a Poor Relationship with Sales

While maintaining a decent relationship with sales is difficult enough, some credit professionals have a more difficult task in this regard. The current relationship with their sales department is poor. This can be due to a prior credit manager or just simply the way it has always been. However, it does not have to continue along a poor path. The credit manager can take the first step and work toward getting the relationship on a better track. We are not going to lie and say that it is easy. It probably won't be. However, it will be worth the effort.

TIPS & TECHNIQUES

Getting the Sales–Credit Relationship Back on Track

- Develop a direct link between sales and credit. Once the sales force perceives the value of its assistance in the collection process, the relationship improves.

- Get sales to feel it is an extension of the credit department. Meet with the salesperson after he or she has visited with key customers to see what was learned. An observant salesperson can pick up quite a bit of information useful to credit.

- Walk a mile in each others' shoes to get an understanding of the problems faced on both sides of the fence.

- Participate in sales meetings, especially those where strategy is set. It might not be a bad idea to only listen the first time or offer only a few minor suggestions.

Don't be discouraged if your first efforts are rebuffed or if progress is slow. This is to be expected. How long it will take to mend the relationship will depend on how badly it was damaged in the first place. One of the best times to start is if a new sales manager is hired. By starting out on a better footing, the relationship will be easier to mend—before bad habits take hold. Review the tips in this section for improving the relationship and also attempt to meet the sales department more than half way.

What Credit Can Do to Help Sales

One of the best things that credit can do for sales is to find ways to help the sales staff. This means not only finding ways to make a sale to a customer not meeting credit standards, but also perhaps finding a sale that the sales department might not find on its own. By extending a helping hand, credit can take a giant step toward getting the sales-credit relationship out of the ring—and getting sales to listen when credit does say no to a potential sale.

Going to Sales Meetings

One of the best ways that credit can get to know sales is to attend sales meetings—and perhaps even make a presentation at these meetings. The credit professionals who have the best relationship with sales are those who find ways to make short, entertaining presentations at the sales conference. At each meeting, pick one or two topics to present to the sales force. Don't ask for several hours. Let's face it. Few salespeople are going to sit through several hours of credit talk. So, pick your topic well, make the presentation as lively and interesting as possible, and remember to keep it short. The KISS (Keep It Simple Silly) approach works best when making presentations to sales.

The sales meeting is also a good time to get to know various salespeople on a personal basis. Spend as much time as possible at these

TIPS & TECHNIQUES

Helping Sales

- Educate the sales force on payment expectations and the consequences of nonpayment or late payment. This approach works extremely well when commission structure is tied to the timing of collections.

- Meet with the customer and salesperson face-to-face to discuss deductions and other past-due items.

- Preapprove new customers, at least for a small limit, before the sales staff spends the time calling on the account and taking an order.

- Provide sales with information regarding potential customers.

- Whenever you run across a magazine or newspaper article about one of your customers, send a copy of it to the salesperson responsible for the account.

- Anticipate the problems and frustrations experienced by sales, and do what you can to help address those issues.

- If you run across information about an existing customer, especially if that data will help sales make an additional sale, send along a copy of it to the appropriate salesperson.

- Offer to do a preliminary credit check on potential customers before the salesperson makes the sales call. This will save sales time if the account does not meet credit standards. It saves the credit manager a lot of headaches not to have to turn down a sale.

- Offer to prequalify large new customers that sales is considering targeting. This will prevent them from wasting time on clients that will not be accepted. It will also prevent them from playing those silly games that some salespeople do in an attempt to slip by a questionable sale at the last moment.

- Offer to search the Internet for information about potential customers for the sales department.

- Share information received at industry trade groups. However, when using this approach be sure that information shared will not violate any of the mandates of the industry group.

events mingling with sales—especially those out-of-towners who are only a voice on the phone.

Don't expect miracles after one sales conference. However, after attending several conferences, making several interesting educational presentations, and getting to know individual salespeople, the relationship will gradually become less contentious.

Educating Sales about Credit

For the most part, salespeople are not malicious. They do not set out to antagonize credit or make sales to lousy customers. They simply do not understand the basics of credit and the full impact of a bad sale. Thus, it usually falls on the shoulders of the credit manager to educate them about these sad financial facts. Once they understand, most are more amenable to abiding by credit's guidelines. The smart credit professional recognizes this fact and sets about educating the sales force, either at the sales meeting or otherwise. Tips & Techniques, "Educating Sales," contains suggestions from other credit professionals that have worked when it comes to educating the sales staff.

TIPS & TECHNIQUES

Educating Sales

- Talk to both the sales force and the customer about asset management. When the sales force understands the impact of time on money, it is less apt to offer extended terms behind credit's back.

- Teach the sales force the importance of following credit guidelines and the financial consequences of ignoring those rules.

- Hold training meeting for sales reps to expose them to credit department policies and procedures. By educating them, it is also possible to enlist their help in providing necessary information up front, thus speeding the approval process.

- Invite the sales manager and any assistants to one of credit's regular meetings, and include them in the details of all credit's activities from the application processing and the percentage approved to the quota of collection calls made each day.

- Setup mini-credit-training sessions for sales so they can get a feel for the work that is done in the credit department.

- Use the field sales staff to contact key personnel that already have a relationship established to get monies released. Convince the sales staff that good cash flow starts with them and it is important to get everything correct when the order is taken.

- Demonstrate to the sales force the dollar amount of sales needed to offset every dollar written off. Many don't realize the huge volume needed to offset each loss.

Involving Sales in the Collection Effort

At most companies, the salesperson has the strongest relationship with the customer. This makes them the best person to collect for the company. However, few salespeople will willingly participate in collection efforts. If at all possible, get the salesperson involved in collections.

Make sales responsible for collecting from those customers not meeting credit standards, if not all customers. This technique is especially effective when the salesperson insists on selling to a shaky customer. If the salesperson insists, make the sale contingent on the salesperson handling the collection effort.

Some companies have success in collections by using the sales force to pick up checks, if necessary. Most salespeople do not like doing this, but customers often have a difficult time refusing to give a check to the salesperson even though they seem to have no problem at all delaying the credit manager. Thus, the technique is particularly effective—if the company is willing to put pressure on the salesperson to participate in the collection of delinquent accounts.

How to Keep Sales from Selling to Noncreditworthy Customers

Remember the old saying in credit that a sale is not a sale until the invoice is collected—until that point it is a gift? Trying to convince some salespeople of this fact is not so easy. Tips & Techniques, "Preventing Sales to Customers Who Don't Meet Your Credit Standards," contains advice from some credit professionals on how they were successful in stopping their sales staffs from selling to customers who were not quite up to credit standards. See if some of the advice might work at your firm.

TIPS & TECHNIQUES

Preventing Sales to Customers Who Don't Meet Your Credit Standards

- Attend senior management meetings and report on accounts receivable status. When management sees firsthand the results of poor credit decisions, they are less likely to side with sales the next time the sales manager goes over your head.

- Begin to measure the sales staff on a return on assets basis.

- Develop delinquency bad-debt write-off reports by salesperson, showing which individuals are responsible for lower quality accounts receivable.

- Establish written credit guidelines that are extremely detailed but allow for some flexibility. When everyone knows what the ground rules are, there are fewer areas for disagreement.

- Notify the sales staff of seriously delinquent accounts so that they may intervene with the customer, if they wish, before the account is put on credit hold.

- Place customers not meeting standards on credit hold quickly if payment is delayed.

- Provide sales with reports that concern their customers. Also, provide all salespeople with delinquency numbers for their customers.

- Provide the sales department with copies of aging reports. Before doing this, however, make sure the report is easy to decipher. Giving the sales force a 100-page computer run defeats the purpose. Condense these voluminous reports into a manageable page or two, highlighting key delinquent items.

TIPS & TECHNIQUES CONTINUED

- Schedule quarterly meetings with the vice president of sales to review days sales outstanding figures and other financial numbers on key accounts.

- Establish a policy where no order can be accepted until the credit application has been completed and approved.

- Have all orders entered through a computer system, which flags accounts on hold. Have the system refuse to accept new orders until the flag is removed. The credit department can only do this withdrawal.

- Insist on having a copy of all purchase orders before goods are shipped.

- Let the sales department know of every invoice that is turned over to a collection agency.

- Make management aware of the potential financial impact of selling to customers who do not meet credit standards.

- Pay commissions after invoices are paid.

- Penalize branch managers' income and hold them accountable for releasing unauthorized goods.

- Provide aging reports to the sales force and bring them into the loop on accounts receivable issues. Giving them information on an ongoing basis means they will not be surprised when credit lines are pulled.

- Send the marketing department a report showing them the status of their accounts.

- Send weekly aging reports to representatives and make them collect on past-due balances. If debt goes past 60 days, no commissions are paid.

- Set the computer program so that it will lock out orders and require approval from credit before an order can be processed.

Summary

The sales department isn't going away. In fact, without them, most companies would not exist and hence most credit professionals would not have their jobs. The savvy credit professional finds a way to establish a good working relationship with sales.

IN THE REAL WORLD

The Credit Game

Having fun and working with sales are two things that don't go together for most credit departments. But not at Cutter & Buck. The company's supervisor of credit and collections, Kelly Simon, shares an interesting tale of how her credit department solved this seemingly impossible dilemma. The sales department had a three-day meeting planned. They wanted the sales staff to meet with different departments to find out about new procedures and ongoing issues. Credit was given a half hour to discuss topics of its choice. It would have to present this material four different times, because the reps would be in small groups and rotate between the different departments. The credit management thought it would be nice to make it more interactive. So they decided it would be fun to play a game called "the credit game."

Several members of the staff came up with the idea to play "Credit Jeopardy" the first time. It had five categories, such as new accounts, collections, and so on, and then had multiple questions for each category. Categories were posted on a corkboard. Buzzers were taken from children's board games for them to "buzz in" with their answers.

When the credit department knows the sales staff will be coming for a meeting, the entire credit department collaborates on a new credit game. They tend to draw questions from those little things that bug them and tend to happen over and over again. The second game the group did was "Credit Family Feud" and most recently "Who Wants to be a Millionaire."

Once sales played the game once, they had so much fun that they were hooked! For the last meeting, there was one group that didn't get to play, and credit heard comment after comment about how disappointed they were.

The benefits seem endless. The sales reps have more fun. Because it is a competitive game (and we all know how much sales reps like to win!), they are more involved. Because they are more involved, they retain more information. Sometimes they like to "cheat" and tell other people the answers, but credit doesn't discourage this. Since they laugh and have a good time, it makes the sales reps feel a greater sense of being on the same team with credit (rather than being on opposing teams), and it gives a sense of bonding between the two departments. Also, it is a great team-building exercise for the credit department. Everyone contributes, not only in the preparation of the game, but also in leading the game. It also is satisfying that the game addresses issues. *Survivor*, anyone?

CHAPTER 7

Customer Relations and Customer Visits

After reading this chapter you will be able to

- Understand the value of customer visits
- Know how to plan a visit to an international customer
- Know what to expect when visiting an international customer
- Find creative ways to make customer visits happen

Most accomplished credit professionals do visit their major customers at least once every few years. Some make it a point to visit at least once a year. At some companies, the importance of this visit is not understood and it is the job of the credit manager to get management to see that these trips bring value to the company and are not simply a boondoggle for the credit professional.

Why Visit a Customer?

There are many good reasons to visit customers. For starters, once there is a personal relationship, the customer is more likely to pay its bills in a timely manner. Additionally, if times are tough, it is likely to be the vendor with the strong relationship that gets paid first rather than the one with the acrimonious one.

Additionally, many credit professionals say that they can learn many things in person that cannot be communicated over the phone or by mail. Often, an inadvertent remark will fall from someone's lips when you spend a little bit of time with them. For starters, when walking through the offices, the credit professional will see whether the offices are in good repair or not. This is something that is more useful after several visits. A company that always kept pristine offices with impeccable landscaping is only likely to let those things go if money is tight.

Another advantage of visiting is that frequently financial statements that never seem to make it to the mail can be picked up. It's not that the customer doesn't want to provide them—they just somehow never get sent.

Customer visits are a good time to resolve disputes, settle unauthorized discounts, and get to know the accounts payable manager at the company.

Customers' Accounts Payable Contact

Many credit professionals overlook the importance of establishing a good relationship with a professional in the customers' accounts payable departments. The value of these relationships should not be underestimated. Since few people bother to treat those in accounts payable as though they mattered, those who do reap the benefits. The accounts payable associates often have the ability to move your payment date up —or schedule it at a later date.

Once you find someone who is helpful, write that person's name and phone number down for future reference. Then, when there is a problem in the future at that company (and you know, it's only a matter of time until there is another problem), contact your trusty reference for a quick resolution. If the individual has been exceedingly helpful, it might not be a bad idea to send a card or small gift at Christmas.

What to Bring

Don't go empty handed to the customer. While your goal is to get to know the people you will be meeting, you will also have some business issues to attend to. You also don't want the customer to ask a question you can't answer, or put you on the spot by providing inaccurate information. For example, if the customer claims it always pays on time, you should be able to whip out your trusty aging report to back up your claims of invoices that are past due. In the best of all worlds, bring:

- A current, detailed statement of the customer's account
- Copies of pertinent correspondence since your last visit
- Ratio trend analysis of their financial picture
- A color chart showing their payment trend over the last 12 months (when the trend is not good)
- Notes you took during your previous credit visit
- Documentation of all disputes that you wish to discuss

With this information you should be armed with the ammunition you need to discuss the customer's account and to refute any inaccurate claims the customer might make.

Don't let the customer put you on the spot. You do not have to answer every question or request that the customer makes, if you do not have adequate information with you. You can get back to them.

How Customer Visits Can Be Made Inexpensively

If the customer is located in the next town or within a 100-mile radius, getting in your car and driving to see the customer is a reasonable way to tackle the issue. Few companies have a problem paying the modest expenses associated with such trips. The difficulty arises when the customer isn't located so conveniently.

Some credit professionals regularly schedule trips to see a number of customers on one visit. If a company has five customers within 50 miles of each other, the credit manager might make a two- or three-day trip to see them all. Similarly, if a route can be planned out to allow the credit manager to see five to ten customers along a particular path, many take this approach, planning a weeklong trip to see these important customers.

Another approach used by many is to incorporate customer visits in other trips. Thus, a credit professional attending an industry group meeting might see customers in the area. The fact that these meetings are often moved around the country gives the credit professional the opportunity to see customers that might not otherwise be visited. Similarly, some credit managers incorporate customer visits when attending credit conferences.

Finally, a few credit managers report that they have been successful in visiting customers while on vacation. Now some reading this might wonder why a credit manager might want to take vacation time to visit a customer for the company. There are several reasons. For starters, some credit professionals truly care about doing a good job—even if it means using some of their personal time. Many who do incorporate visits on a vacation simply tack on a workday. Others get their company to pay for part of the vacation—usually either the airfare or the hotel room for one or two nights. For some credit professionals, using one of their vacation days to visit customers is the first step toward getting the company to pay for customer visits in the future.

It should be noted that even if the credit professional does use vacation time for the visit, the company still typically pays for any meals that the credit manager might have with the customer.

Who Goes on **Customer Visits**

When a credit professional goes on a customer visit, the credit staff does not go along. Typically, the salesperson might accompany the credit manager for the area, the area manager, a financial person or the credit professional might simply go alone. It depends on the company, the credit manager, the corporate culture, and what the company is attempting to accomplish on the visit. Some companies will send a new credit manager with a retiring one to visit customers and be introduced.

There are no hard and fast rules as to who goes on a customer visit and what is to be accomplished. Each company can set its own agenda.

Customer Visits: **Unscheduled**

There are times when customer visits will be called for apart from the normal routine. A few examples are:

- From time to time, every credit professional will have one or more customers with deteriorating financials. A thorough financial analysis may suggest that the credit limit be reduced especially if the payment history is deteriorating.

- Occasionally, a salesperson will bring in an unusually large order from an existing customer. If orders from this firm had been small in the past, a thorough credit review may not have been done and may be required quickly. This might necessitate a quick visit to the customer.

- Occasionally, especially when selling internationally, the salesperson might bring in a large order on which the credit manager is not comfortable offering open account terms. A trip to the customer with the salesperson might be called for to develop another method of selling—say on a secured basis.

- A rush order from a new customer definitely merits close scrutiny. A visit to the customer might be in order.

Customer Visits: A Reality Check

Having pointed out all the benefits of customer visits, we are now forced to concede that many companies do not send their credit professionals on these trips. While they only make sense when large dollars are at stake, the number of trips actually taken by credit professionals to see customers is not as large as it should be.

At one meeting of international credit professionals, the question was raised. Approximately 20% of those in attendance visited their international customers on a regular basis. This is a shame because, especially when selling internationally, the opportunity for a misunderstanding is great. Customer visits are a great way to resolve disputes and misinterpretations and break new ground. It also provides an opportunity for the international credit professional to begin to understand the culture in which the customer operates.

While more companies are willing to send credit professionals to see customers domestically, the number that actually does is probably not greater than 50%.

TIPS & TECHNIQUES

Your First International Trip

Preparing for an overseas credit trip can be an intimidating experience, even for experienced international credit professionals. Paul Beretz, an experienced international professional and a principal of Pacific Business Solutions, shares his expertise on international customer visits, which he strongly advocates for anyone selling internationally. While he concedes such trips are expensive—both in terms of money and time—he urges pressing this with management. Both the company and the credit manager will benefit tremendously.

Based on his 20-plus years of international credit experience, Beretz offers 18 tips to help make such trips as productive as possible. These guidelines are useful for those traveling for the first time or the fiftieth. His advice includes:

1. *Don't leave your preparation for the trip to the plane ride.* "It's a big mistake," Beretz cautions. For starters, unless you're riding in business class, you'll be cramped for space and won't get much work done. Even if you're fully relaxed, you won't be able to do anything about missing information and reports.

2. *Better to stay late a few nights before your trip and get your itinerary, important papers, and reports together.* That way, you'll have time to gather all the information you need. Once you're on the plane, there's nothing that can be done about lost or missing data.

3. *When planning the trip, define your objectives.* Write down what you are trying to achieve. Be very specific in the details. This will serve as a useful reminder and ensure that you don't forget anything.

4. *Get input from internal customers.* These are your own product and country specialists. Find out, beforehand, what your company's competitive position is with the customer you are visiting. This information will help you come across with confidence.

5. *Use your bankers and certified public accounting (CPA) firms to develop information on what's going on in the country where you will be doing business.* These professionals can help you establish contacts in your customer's country.

TIPS & TECHNIQUES CONTINUED

6 *Use the bankers as a firsthand source of information regarding the difficulty of getting funds out of the country to which you are exporting.* This may or may not be an issue, but if the currency is blocked, or partially blocked, you will want to knowthis before you ship. In such instances, you may be able to make other arrangements.

7 *Be realistic about your time.* Allow time for delays, layovers, and other transportation difficulties. Don't schedule your first meeting right after you land. If your plane is even a little late, you'll be behind before you even get started.

8 *Have a contingency plan if the person who is supposed to pick you up is not there when you land.* This is especially important if you are going to a country where you do not speak the language.

9 *Always carry with you the local phone number of someone you know in the country.* Have your destination address faxed to you in advance. Make sure the fax is in both English and the native language, so if you are forced to rely on a taxi or other means of public transportation, you can show the fax to the driver.

10 *Be wary of fatigue.* A business trip is not the time to experiment with foods you've never eaten before. If your trip includes a weekend, as it very well may, take time off. Don't try to schedule business meetings. Give yourself a break. If you like, do a little sightseeing—with the emphasis on little.

11 *Get a good country analysis before you go.* This way you'll have the political lay of the land before you arrive.

12 *Laptops are great for working on the plane or back in your hotel room at night.* However, as anyone who has ever lugged one around can attest, they can get heavy very quickly. If you still decide to take one along, make sure to carry the invoice for the machine. This is imperative if you are traveling to the Pacific Rim. The purpose of the invoice is so when leaving the country, you will be able to prove that you did not buy the computer while visiting.

⑬ *Allow for canceled meetings.* In order to get the maximum return out of your trip, have some backup plans in case one of your contacts can't meet with you as originally arranged. These plans can be as simple as visiting with your local employees.

⑭ *Send along a copy of your written agenda to the local branch of your company before your visit.* This should be fairly detailed and should include the names of the people you are planning to see, when you will be seeing them, and what you are going to do. Additionally, it should clearly identify who is supposed to do what. Get their concurrence with your plans and itinerary. Ask them for suggestions. At all costs, avoid the "we're from headquarters and we're here to help" approach.

⑮ *Be up-to-date on your company, products, and the country you are visiting.* This education will help you understand the problems of those you meet while making you appear the informed executive you strive to be.

⑯ *While it is almost always more advantageous rate-wise to exchange U.S. currency for local denominations upon arrival, consider converting from $50 to $100 at the departing U.S. airport.* This will allow for situations where offshore airport money exchange centers are closed and provide you—in most cases—"walk-around money" or taxi fare until you arrive at your hotel.

⑰ *Have credit cards appropriate for the destination country by confirming acceptance with your travel planner.*

⑱ *Do not depend on overseas automated teller machines (ATMs) to obtain local currency.* You may be disappointed,

TIPS & TECHNIQUES CONTINUED

despite assurances from your travel planner that the ATM card of choice will work in the overseas location.

(19) *While seemingly obvious, realize that there are always things that can be learned regardless of whether the traveler is a novice or a veteran.*

When in Rome...

Before setting out to visit customers in another country, it might be a good idea to learn a little about that country—its customs, language, and culture. This is not as difficult as it might seem at first glance. There are a number of books that provide this information. They include:

- *Do's and Taboos Around the World.* Roger E. Axtell (editor). New York: John Wiley & Sons, Inc., 1993.

- *Kiss, Bow, or Shake Hands: How to Do Business in 60 Countries.* Terri Morrison, Wayne A. Conaway, and George A. Borden. Avon, MA: Adams Media Company, 1994.

- *Do's and Taboos Around the World for Women in Business.* Roger E. Axtell (editor), et al. New York: John Wiley & Sons, Inc.,1997.

- *Dun & Bradstreet's Guide to Doing Business Around the World.* Terri Morrison, Wayne A. Conaway, and Joseph J. Douress. Paramus, NJ: Prentice Hall Press, 2000.

- *Do's and Taboos of Humor Around the World: Stories and Tips from Business and Life.* Roger E. Axtell. New York: John Wiley & Sons, Inc., 1998.

- *Gestures: The Do's and Taboos of Body Language Around the World.* Roger E. Axtell and Mike Fornwald (illustrator). New York: John Wiley & Sons, Inc., 1997.

- *International Business Etiquette, Latin America: What You Need to Know to Conduct Business Abroad With Charm and Savvy.* Ann Marie Sabath. Franklin Lakes, NJ: Career Press, Inc., 1999.

In addition to providing excellent information, many of these books are also quite entertaining.

IN THE REAL WORLD

Personal Visits Help Credit Pro Save His Company from a Collection Disaster

Relationships with companies in other countries often start small and gradually grow into larger ones. This can be an ideal way to develop a relationship if the proper care is taken every step of the way. Lose control or fail to make needed adjustments in time, though, and you can end up with nothing to show for your efforts. A credit manager for an East Coast producer of poultry feed ingredients selling in the Dominican Republic relates his experiences with a collection problem his company is having with its distributor, how he is attempting to solve it, and what could have been done differently to avoid the problems in the first place.

The Story

"A small local supplier to the retail food and poultry production industries in the Dominican Republic became our distributor in 1992 at a time when we had only two or three end-user customers there," the credit manager explains. "No formal agreement was executed until early 1997 by which time the distributor had grown our business to include some 43 end users...small feed mills and farmers growing broilers throughout the island. All along, it was verbally agreed that this was not our exclusive distributor even though we never sold to other local distributors.

IN THE REAL WORLD CONTINUED

"Foreign suppliers to the Dominican Republic should become knowledgeable of Law 173, which gives local distributors and agents serious protection provided they register their foreign supplier with the Central Bank within 60 days after the first shipment arrives in the Dominican Republic. The financial penalty can be heavy if the foreign supplier eventually terminates the commercial relationship under almost any circumstances.

"From the beginning, the distributor paid us slow and shared financial statements on a very irregular basis. Payment terms were quasi-consignment in that we shipped large containers full of our drummed liquid product directly to the distributor who was then supposed to remit partial payments in U.S. dollars to us 60 days after it made small, daily deliveries to the individual end users. This became a bookkeeping nightmare for the distributor, but its limited financial resources made single large payments to us impossible. Total credit risk and devaluation exposure rested with the distributor who invoiced and collected from end users in Dominican pesos."

Collection Solutions

Not happy with the payment history, this savvy credit professional tried several approaches. Two of the strategies he tried are:

❶ By 1997, he was accepting five or six postdated checks to cover a single invoice with final settlement stretching out four or five months after bill of lading (B/L) date.

❷ The two principals then personally guaranteed four *pagares* due "on demand" totaling US $200,000, which was the approved credit limit.

He also visited with the debtor several times to try to make the relationship work. This credit professional believes that these visits helped promote a personal relationship with the debtor and helped keep the matter from deteriorating further.

IN THE REAL WORLD CONTINUED

"After a few of these checks were returned nonsufficient funds by Cayman banks, my company stopped shipping, and the end users were left with no choice but to buy from our competitors," he continues. "Since late 1997, the distributor has complained that our pricing was too high for it to earn a profit. Our knowledge of the local poultry market confirmed this; however, many months passed before a needed price adjustment was seriously considered.

"The distributor's last checks cleared the banks in early 1998, after which a small bank transfer was received in mid December. Several pay plans were negotiated during 1997 to 1998 but all have ended in default, due in part to our delay with a price adjustment. Now, both parties appear anxious to end the relationship and part company without burning bridges.

"The outstanding and past-due balance is almost US $290,000, versus the US $100,000 our distributor proposes as a fair settlement in view of its efforts to develop the local market and earn a decent profit these past seven years. Local attorneys are in the picture, consulting, but we are hopeful a settlement fair to both sides can be negotiated without litigation in the Dominican Republic."

Lessons Learned

"One result of all this has been a realization that you are always better off if you can service and sell directly to your end customers," says this weary credit executive. "Distributors, no doubt, offer many sales and financial advantages, but they quickly become a barrier between you and your customers. In most countries, terminating a distributor usually results in severe financial costs for the foreign suppliers. Take great care in selecting your distributors and try to have more than one in a given country...if just to defend against an eventual claim of exclusivity.

"Personal visits also are important when trying to resolve this mess, versus attempting to solve it with phone calls or with faxes

Summary

Customer visits are just one tool in the arsenal of tools used by a competent credit professional. Many companies are reluctant to pay the costs of such trips. However, when the value of these exchanges is fully understood, their value quickly becomes apparent. If at all possible, credit professionals should search for creative ways to make these visits happen.

CHAPTER 8

Letters of Credit and Other Security Interests

After reading this chapter you will be able to

- Understand the proper use of letters of credit
- Take the appropriate steps to avoid the problems that typically plague the use of letters of credit
- Use Uniform Commercial Code (UCC)-1 filings in the appropriate manner to guard your firm's security interests
- Identify other appropriate techniques to use to sell when open account is not an option

Remember, it is the credit department's job to find a way to make a sale happen even if the customer has less than sterling credit. When selling on open account is not advisable, and the customer is reluctant to pay cash-in-advance, suppliers look for some other guarantee. This chapter focuses on some of the more common alternatives to open-account terms.

Techniques to Secure Your Position with Risky Customers

When open account is not feasible, companies look for ways to secure their position and limit losses. Some ask for a partial payment in advance. This approach works well especially for those selling a high-margin product. Those companies can require a payment in advance that covers their costs. Then if the customer doesn't pay, the company isn't actually out of pocket. However, partial payment in advance for high-margin product will only work for a small percentage of companies. The rest will need to find another way to secure their position. A few techniques that work are:

- *Letters of credit.* These can either be standby or documentary. The important thing to remember about letters of credit is that they are about documents, not facts. The major difference is that the documentary letter of credit is intended as a payment mechanism, while the standby only comes into play when there is a default in fact by the debtor. While many view standby letters of credit as guarantees, they technically are not. The reason for this is that, in many jurisdictions, banks are prohibited from issuing guarantees but may issue standby letters of credit. Letters of credit are discussed in more detail later in this chapter.

- *Security interest.* These are liens covering goods sold by creditors to customers or liens covering all of the customer's assets, including accounts receivable, inventory, equipment, and general intangibles. The interest is created by obtaining a security agreement describing the collateral, which is perfected by recording a UCC financing statement in proper form. Filing the financing statement (unless proceeds are expressly excluded) automatically covers the proceeds. Security interests are discussed in detail later in this chapter.

- *Guaranty.* Most customers are loath to offer a personal guaranty unless there is no other way they can get the sale done. Yet getting a personal guarantee is one of the best ways to secure payment as few guarantors are going to willingly put themselves in a position where you can come after them for payment. Generally speaking, these can either be corporate or individual. Typically for credit issues, the guaranty used is one for payment.

The guaranty of collection, used much less frequently, requires that the creditor exhaust all legal remedies against the customer before proceeding against the guarantor. Credit professionals should be aware that Federal Reserve Regulation B states that demanding the guarantee of a spouse is unenforceable and subject to penalty, unless the spouse is involved in the business or substantially owns assets or has joint ownership. If you take a personal guarantee, make sure to note it in your files and keep the signed documentation in a secure location.

- *Mechanics liens.* This will not be applicable to all reading this publication, but will be very useful in those instances where it works. *Barron's Finance & Investment Handbook* defines a mechanics lien as follows: "a lien against buildings or other structures, allowed by some states to contractors, laborers and suppliers of materials used in their construction or repair. The lien remains in effect until these people have been paid in full and may, in the event of a liquidation before they have been paid, give them priority over other creditors."

- *Joint checks.* This approach is often used in the construction industry, but some credit professionals report success in using this approach with weaker or smaller distributors. A check could be issued from the end user to the supplier and the distributor. This approach takes a little extra work, and often the distributor will balk. However, if it is the only way to get the transaction completed, the distributor may have no choice.

What Is a Letter of Credit?

Barron's Dictionary of Finance and Investment Terms defines a letter of credit as "an instrument or document issued by a bank guaranteeing the payment of a customer's drafts up to a stated amount for a specified period. It substitutes the bank's credit for the buyer's and eliminates the seller's risk." Thus, it is imperative that the bank's credit meets your company's credit standards. To meet your company's needs, the letter of credit must be filled out accurately and correctly. If there is one small error, the bank will deem the letter of credit discrepant and send the letter of credit back to you to get it fixed. If it cannot be adjusted within the dated time frame, it expires and the company is in the same situation as if it had sold on open account. This situation is not desirable since the reason most suppliers go to the time and expense of getting a letter of credit is that they do not want to sell on open-account terms.

Specifically, the letter of credit should:

- Be irrevocable
- Be dated
- Specify the beneficiary and the account party
- Specify the amount
- Be numbered
- Be issued on bank stationery
- Be signed
- Allow drafts at specific tenors to be drawn on the bank
- List the documents required

Missing any one of these items can make the letter of credit unusable. When the letter of credit has a problem, the bank will send it back to the beneficiary (i.e., your company) to be fixed. Of course, the bank charges a fee for this. Some credit professionals assert that the reason banks are so picky about letters of credit is that they want the fees associated with fixing discrepant items. Needless to say, the banks deny this. More to the point, the banks do not want to be in a position where they have paid out on an inaccurate letter of credit. It is the painstaking nature of letters of credit combined with the nitpicking nature of banks that cause many credit professionals to hate letters of credit.

Types of Letters of Credit

All letters of credit are not the same. There are several types each with its own purpose including the following:

- *Standby letters of credit.* This type of letter of credit is used most frequently to guarantee the performance or for services. They can be found backing bonds, loans, or future interest payments. They are put in place as a type of insurance with the intent that they never be drawn. However, if the underlying obligation is not met, the letter of credit can, and often is, drawn upon by the beneficiary. The bank honoring the obligation will then either debit the bank account of the issuer or convert the obligation into a loan.

- *Revolving letters of credit.* These letters of credit are typically used in those instances where there is repeat business. By obtaining one letter of credit to handle multiple shipments, the administrative work with the bank is reduced. Limits can be placed on the amount and the timing of each draw. In these instances, it is intended that the letters of credit be drawn against. In order to do so, the seller presents the specified documents to the bank. Monitoring of such letters of credit is of vital importance as a missed date can mean not getting paid on a timely basis.

- *Deferred payment letters of credit.* This letter of credit is similar in many respects to a revolving one except that payment does not take place immediately. It is used in those cases where the seller agrees to offer extended terms to the buyer. With this type of letters of credit, the seller presents documents to the bank as soon as it receives them but does not receive payment until some agreed-upon date in the future. Besides the security feature, there is the advantage of having such a letter of credit over selling on open account. The seller can use the bank's promise of future payment to obtain credit from its own bank, effectively trading on the credit of the bank that issued the letter of credit. The period of deferment usually exceeds six months making this an attractive instrument in only a few cases—usually those involving heavy machinery.

- *Transferable letters of credit.* When the seller of goods is actually only acting as an intermediary, it may be necessary to have a letter of credit transferable in order to complete the transaction. This is not typically allowed with letters of credit. However, it is possible to have the document marked as transferable. In these instances, the rights are passed on to the transferee (of which there can be more than one). All transferees must comply with the terms and conditions spelled out in the original letter of credit.

    Usually, before any transfer is made, the beneficiary must send a request in writing to the bank to effect such a transfer. This is one more step in a process filled with paper and details. It also presents another opportunity for discrepancies to creep into the documents and another opening for banks to bounce those not properly completed. This will inevitably add time to the process. Those considering using this type of letters of credit should factor this into their time equation and make sure the letter of credit is issued for a long enough period to cover delays.

    Many banks will not make these transfers until they have been paid for their services—another cause for delay. Most experts recommend that when such letters of credit are used, the dates should be prior to, and the amounts less than, the date and the amount of the original letter of credit. Some experts refer to transferable letters of credit as assignable letters of credit. The two are the same. While the use of this type of letter of credit can often add complications to an already complex process, it is sometimes unavoidable. By knowing the possible weak points, the credit manager will be able to gain the most from these letters of credit.

- *Back-to-back letters of credit.* This type of letter of credit is usually preferable to a transferable letter of credit—although banks are not generally thrilled with this type of an arrangement either. Again, it is often used by a middle man, typically one that might have trouble obtaining credit based on their own financials. With back-to-backs, the intermediary will ask a bank to issue a second letter of credit in favor of the ultimate supplier, using the letter of credit issued by the buyer as collateral for the second one.

  In this arrangement, the terms and conditions of both letters of credit are identical except the amounts and dates in the second one must be smaller and earlier. The risk with this is the performance of the original letter of credit is contingent on the timely and perfect execution of the second. Those using such instruments are advised to ensure there is plenty of time allowed for delays.

A Little Bit of Letters of Credit History

How long have letters of credit been in use? Answer the question before reading on. John W. Dunlop, president of AVG Trade Group, a company specializing in letters of credit management, documents, and payment via the Internet, answers the question. "Letters of credit," he says, "are one of the oldest trade tools, having their genesis when King John of England ordered marble from Italy in 1210 with a 'credit letter.'"

Why You Should Review Letters of Credit Early

Whoever first said "the early bird gets the worm" was probably not thinking about letters of credit, but it is certainly an apt expression in this area. Early review of letters of credit will not ensure that you will get paid under the letter of credit, but it will dramatically improve your chances.

Ideally, the letter of credit should be reviewed before the transaction is completed. However, the reality, as most people reading this are aware, is that few have that luxury. Thus, they are stuck playing catch-up once the documents arrive. Reviewing letters of credit is such a tedious task that it is tempting to note the due date and then toss it into a drawer to be retrieved a day or two before it needs to be presented to the bank. However, this can be a big mistake. Some things that can go wrong if you wait until the last minute are:

- *Timing problems.* Obviously, if there is a problem in the letter of credit and it needs to be changed, waiting until the last minute will not permit adequate time for the letter of credit to be fixed. However, that is only the beginning of the timing problems that can arise.

    Letters of credit have an expiration date, and occasionally they are written in such a way that the date does not give the seller adequate time to meet the conditions spelled out in the letter of credit. Should this happen, the seller is effectively left at the mercy of the buyer when it comes to payment. Since letters of credit are typically used with customers to whom you did not wish to give open-account terms, this can be a problem, since this is what you are left with if the letter of credit expires without being presented.

- *Discrepancy problems.* It is not possible to talk about letters of credit without addressing the nasty issue of discrepancies. Most experts estimate that anywhere from 80 to 90% of them have discrepancies, which need to be fixed. The earlier in the process the problems are uncovered, the more likely they are to be fixed on time. It is not uncommon to hear stories of buyers with real or imagined quality issues with the goods using a discrepancy in the letter of credit to negate the contract and renegotiate the price of the goods.

- *Compliance problems.* Even those who do check letters of credit early on in the game to uncover discrepancy problems sometimes forget to take the process one more step. It is important to make sure that it is possible to comply with all the documentary requirements in the letter of credit. It does little good to have a letter of credit with no discrepancies if the company cannot comply with it.

  However, determining if conditions can be met is often beyond the scope of the credit professional—especially when it comes to the business and shipping side of the transaction. Prudent credit managers send copies of their letters of credit to every department involved in the transaction to ensure that the conditions can be met. This often includes the outside freight forwarder.

  By compelling everyone involved to check their portions, you will increase the odds of being in compliance. Do not, however, assume that since someone has not replied, everything is satisfactory. Require a positive or negative response. Checking letters of credit should not be a case of "Regrets Only."

TIPS & TECHNIQUES

16 Ways to Use a Standby Letter of Credit

Letters of credit can be used in many innovative ways. Some of the ways innovative credit professionals have found to make sales happen by using a letter of credit are:

1 To guarantee that payment will be made or performance of certain requirements will be completed after a contract or bid has been awarded

2 To advance funds to the seller by the purchaser for the purchase of materials for a project

3 To back up the obligations of the seller should it not perform in accordance with the conditions outlined in a contract

4 To provide assurance during a warranty period that a project will run smoothly after completion

5 To back up underwriting obligations

6 To allow a company to self-insure for potential workers' compensation claims

7 To collateralize a loan repayment or interest payments when, without the letter of credit, the loan might not have been given or a higher interest rate might have been charged

8 To securitize a company's accrued vacation liability in order to accelerate the expense on its financial statements

9 To help companies with local bid requirements for guarantees issued on the strength of the issuing bank's letter of credit in foreign countries

10 To help companies backstop their environmental cleanup liabilities

11 To improve the credit ratings of securities, bonds, notes, or commercial paper supported by a letter of credit

12 To mitigate portfolio risk when securitizing assets

13 To encourage investment in an area by enabling companies to access less costly tax-exempt financing

14 To subsidize investment in equipment that will protect the environment with tax-exempt financing

15 To backstop a state's obligation when it issues notes that will later be repaid through taxation and also to provide a liquidity facility

16 To back up a commercial paper program that will provide low-cost, short-term financing and a liquidity facility, often enabling the program to obtain a higher-quality rating than it might have been able to obtain without the letter of credit

Since letters of credit are about documents and not facts, the inability to produce a given document at the correct time will negate the letter of credit—effectively putting the transaction right back on open-account terms. The odds of producing a perfect letter of credit with no errors are greatly improved if you start reviewing the documents as early in the process as you possibly can.

Security Interests

Creditors concerned about getting paid by a particular debtor will sometimes agree to sell to that customer if they can take a purchase money security interest in the collateral. This allows the creditor to achieve a first priority position in the collateral should the debtor file for bankruptcy protection. Unfortunately, the steps that one had to take to properly achieve this priority position were complicated and the slightest mistake in the filings could invalidate the priority. All that changed on July 1, 2001. Speaking at Reimer Week, Bill Creim and Jane Fennelly, attorneys with Creim, Cacias & Koenig LLP, explained the new procedures and why credit managers who had previously avoided this process might want to reconsider.

Background

"A security interest is a type of lien taken by a creditor in personal property of a debtor," explains Creim. The process typically includes the following steps:

1. The creditor has the debtor sign a Security Agreement.

2. The creditor files a UCC-1 financing statement.

The security agreement is a contract between the debtor and creditor in which the debtor grants the creditor a lien against specific collateral held by the debtor. This agreement establishes the creditor's rights against the debtor.

The UCC-1 financing statement filing perfects its security interest and establishes the creditor's rights in the debtor's collateral against all other creditors of the debtor.

A creditor who takes a security interest in the inventory it sells to the debtor is said to have a Purchase Money Security Interest in that inventory, hence the term PMSI.

The section of the UCC that deals with security interests is Article 9. Before the revisions, the filings had to be done in all states where the collateral was located and in some cases, in certain counties, as well. This provision alone kept many credit professionals from taking security interests, but that has changed as you'll read further on.

Why Take a Security Interest?

For starters, taking a security interest will allow a creditor to sell to a company that does not meet its credit standards or it will allow the credit manager to extend additional credit. Creim gives the example of the credit manager who tells the sales manager that she will offer a $100,000 line without a security interest but will increase the line to $200,000 if the debtor agrees to a security interest. This should help ease relations with the sales department.

There is another reason for taking a security interest. If a bankruptcy filing occurs, the filing gives the creditor a possible defense against a preference attack.

Given the elimination of the multiple filing requirements, the process has become much simpler and in many cases less expensive. Those who objected to the cost no longer have this complaint.

The Changes

Creim and Fennelly enumerated the key changes as follows:

- The place of filing for UCC financing statements will be based on where the debtor is organized or registered—not the location of the collateral. The speakers point out that filings against sole proprietors should be done in the state of the sole proprietor's principal residence.

- County and multiple filing requirements are eliminated for most types of collateral.

- In some states, UCC filings can be done online.

- The debtor's signature is not required on the UCC filing if the creditor has "authenticated" the grant of the security interest.

- Priority rules become complicated: A creditor may need to search several states to determine its priority in the debtor's collateral.

- The *dual status* approach is approved. A creditor may take a PMSI and a broader security interest.

To see how one credit professional's life has become easier under the new law, see the In the Real World, "A Credit Manager's Life before and after the Revisions to Article 9."

If You Have Existing Filings

The speakers pointed out that taking the following five steps will maximize existing interests.

1. Determine the state of incorporation for all debtors that are corporations or limited liability corporations. Creditors should also verify the state of principal residence for its sole proprietor debtors. Do not assume that it is the same as the state in which the business is located.

2. Determine each debtor's identification number. This number is not the tax identification number. You can get this information from the debtor or from the debtor's state of incorporation.

3. File UCCs in any states where a new filing is required to perfect the security interest. For example, if the creditor has no current filings in the debtor's state of incorporation, file now. Think Delaware. File "in-lieu-of" filings to keep your priority from other states.

4. Update your form security agreement to include authentication language so that you can make future filings without having to obtain the debtor's signature.

5. Consider including a debtor grant of security interest and authentication language in your company's credit application, dealer agreements, and the like.

A Few Other Issues

While most experts believe that ultimately all states will adopt the changes to Article 9, to date a few are dragging their feet. Specifically, Alabama, Connecticut, Florida, and Mississippi have postponed implementation. Thus, if you are doing business in these states, the old rules still applied as of July 1, 2001. Hopefully by the time you are reading this, the states in which you do business will have changed.

IN THE REAL WORLD

A Credit Manager's Life before and after the Revisions to Article 9

The Problem: Joe Credit works for Widgetmaster, Inc. Widgetmaster sells widgets to Debtco, Inc., a company incorporated in Delaware. It does business in 37 states, but not Delaware.

The Solution—Before July 1, 2001: Joe needed to:

- File UCC-1 financing statements in all 37 states where Debtco does business, in addition to extra county filings in many states, to perfect its security interest.

- Conduct UCC searches in all 37 states plus relevant counties.

- Review all the search results and give purchase money notification to all creditors with prior perfected security interests covering Widgetmaster, Inc.'s inventory.

The Solution—After July 1, 2001: Joe will only need to file a UCC-1 financing statement against Debtco with the state of Delaware. *Note:* Remember UCC filings are good for five years. So, until June 30, 2006, Joe will need to conduct a UCC search in Delaware and the other 37 states to determine where to send purchase money notification letters.

The speakers were questioned about getting the debtor's identification number. Like the legal name of the debtor, it is not a good idea to rely on the salesperson for this information. The burden is on the creditor to obtain this information and to use the correct data on all filings. If not, the filing could be invalid and your security interest out the window. Creim suggests asking to see the articles of incorporation of the debtor, as it should have a state stamp with the new number.

Finally, you need to be aware that debtors can and occasionally do terminate filings.

By following the excellent advice offered by the speakers you will be in a good position to decide if taking a security interest under revised Article 9 would benefit your company. Once you have decided to go forward, the advice of the speakers will get you started.

Summary

There are numerous ways to extend credit without putting your company at risk. The ideas presented in this chapter provide an overview of the approaches credit managers can take to secure their company's position.

CHAPTER 9

Legal Considerations Surrounding Credit

After reading this chapter you will be able to

- Understand the laws that affect the credit function
- Identify potential fraud situations
- Make intelligent decisions about escheat issues
- Understand the possibilities of alternative disputer resolution

L et me start out by saying that this chapter is simply an overview of some of the legal aspects affecting the credit profession. It is not meant as an offering of legal advice, but rather to get the reader on the path of thinking of the legal issues that might affect their credit decisions. Readers are advised to consult their own legal counsel regarding these and any other legal issues affecting their credit decisions.

Additionally, the reader should note that the laws that affect credit are continually changing. Thus, it is imperative that as part of your job you follow these issues. The National Association of Credit Managers (NACM) is a good place to start. Also, changes in the bankruptcy laws might affect the way you handle credit. There was much talk in 2001 about revising the bankruptcy law. However, between the deteriorating economy and the events of September 11, lawmakers decided to focus their attention elsewhere and the legislation died—at least temporarily.

At some point in the future the issue will be raised again and credit and collection professionals should follow the issue.

A Review of the Laws that Affect Credit Professionals Today

Are you aware that if you, in your capacity as a credit manager, do not follow the regulations set forth in the Sherman Anti-Trust Act, you could be subject to jail time? Also, did you know that although you won't risk prison by not following the Robinson-Patman Act your company could be subject to triple damages? While many credit managers are knowledgeable about laws affecting the profession, a few are a bit ambiguous. Remember those boring history lessons in high school— the ones you quickly forgot after the test. They are now relevant. Here is a quick review, along with a brief discussion of what you can and cannot do.

Robinson-Patman Act

The Robinson-Patman Act deals with price discrimination between like classes of customers. Before deciding that you do not have to read about this because the credit department does not set prices, realize that the courts have ruled that terms of sale are part of pricing. Thus, discounts offered to one customer must be offered to all customers in the same class.

Some companies have gotten creative in the ways they have tried to disguise pricing discrimination. Promotional payments, allowances, discounts, or services not made available to all competing buyers on proportionally equal terms are all techniques that are considered discriminatory.

The Act also prohibits kickbacks and certain price concessions that occasionally masquerade as brokerage fees.

The penalties for violating Robinson-Patman do not include prison time. However, the financial implications can be quite severe.

Exceptions to Robinson-Patman

At first glance, the constraints of Robinson-Patman seem to make it impossible for a company to compete today. There's hardly a credit manager alive who has not heard a salesperson plead that he or she must meet the competition or a particular order will go to the other company. The federal government is not completely unreasonable. The above scenario is one of three exceptions to Robinson-Patman, but let's be clear about it: Prices, including terms, can be changed on a case-by-case basis to meet competition but not to beat it. This distinction must be kept in mind whenever extended terms are offered to one or two customers, but not all.

The second exception has to do with customized goods. If the product is customized to the extent that there is only one buyer for it, a case can be made that this one customer represents one class and no other companies are in the same class.

Finally, it is allowable to pass along cost savings to customers.

Sherman Act

The Sherman Act regulates antitrust activity and restraint of trade. The rules apply not only to written contracts but also to other express agreements. The part that tends to get credit professionals in trouble is that various forms of conduct or behavior that might evidence an implicit agreement or understanding between two or more groups are covered. This is one of the reasons industry credit groups so scrupulously take notes during meetings. The Act also forbids activities that are deemed to be anticompetitive. These include group boycotts and predatory pricing.

The penalties for violating the Sherman Anti-Trust Act can be severe. For starters, jail time up to one year is possible. Additionally, fines up to $300,000 may be imposed. These penalties are not assessed against the corporation, but rather the individual accused of breaking the law.

Clayton Act

Passed in 1914, 24 years after the Sherman Act, the Clayton Act tightened some of the perceived loopholes in the Sherman. It dealt with local price discrimination and went further in legislating against restraint of trade. It addressed whether certain conduct may have the probable result of substantially lessening competition. Violations of this act can also result in jail time for the offender.

Equal Credit Opportunity Act

A good number of credit professionals think that this applies only to consumer credit, but that is not the case. It is illegal to discriminate against any creditor in any aspect of a credit transaction on the basis of sex, marital status, race, national origin, religion, or age. If a creditor asks in writing why credit was declined, you must respond. Keep records of your actions. Some even recommend sending a written declination along with the reason the credit was denied.

Miller Act

Likely to affect only a small number of credit managers, the Miller Act is for those in the construction industry. Its intent is to protect the U.S. government from mechanics liens. The Act requires that a payment bond be supplied on every federal contract where the price is more than $100,000. The bond is used to guarantee payments to suppliers of goods and services to the project. It also sets stringent parameters as to the timing and procedures for actions covering payments under the bond.

What Credit Managers Need to Do

Becoming aware of the laws that affect the profession provides a good start toward protecting yourself and your company. Then avoid putting yourself in a precarious position.

Be careful what you say when speaking with other credit professionals. The biggest potential problems could occur at industry credit meetings. However, the professional associations do a wonderful job in monitoring these meetings to ensure that no laws are broken. Problems for credit professionals can arise during informal meetings after the official meeting.

The safest guideline for such discussions is that credit professionals limit themselves to conversations about what happened in the past and refuse to talk about the future—even if that future is tomorrow.

When giving trade references, never talk about what credit limits you are likely to give or any changes you are likely to make based on past performance—or lack thereof. Many credit professionals insist that requests for credit references be made in writing, and they provide a bare bones written reference in return. Often their legal department has reviewed the form of this reference. Others take this caution one step further and refuse to supply references at all. This is an unfortunate choice.

Credit professionals who are aware of what the technicalities of the law are and who watch what they say will run little risk of breaking the laws discussed above.

Robinson-Patman Technicalities

Potential Robinson-Patman violations can often occur innocently when no malice is intended. Any favoritism for one customer over another can potentially be viewed as a violation of Robinson-Patman. This is something that few, if any, salespeople ever focus on. Thus, it is important that the credit professional make it very clear to the salespeople that manipulating terms, and other terms of sale, has to be done very carefully or the potential for legal action can exist.

Now the first thing the salesperson is likely to point out is that it would be difficult for anyone to catch these violations, and they could be correct. However, the fact that the likelihood of being caught is low does not mean that the credit professional wants to put the company at risk for a few dollars. Point out the potential and document your warning. It is management's prerogative to override your caution. If they chose to do so, they must be willing to bear the consequences.

Fraud

It does happen. Whether it be in a formal planned out manner, such as a bust-out, or when a customer gets into financial trouble, credit professionals must be on the alert. It is one of the very good reasons for participating in an industry credit group. Here's what can (and does) happen. A customer gets into financial difficulty. It buys widgets from several different suppliers, one of which is your company. This particular supplier has been paying your company within terms, so you are not concerned. In fact, this customer's payment history is so good you don't even bother doing an annual credit review. A quick review of its purchasing history shows that orders from this company have been increasing. Is there anything to worry about?

The answer to this question is maybe. If you've done a credit review and the financials look good and no one in your industry credit group is having payment problems with this company, it is probably okay. However, if you haven't done the credit review and you don't go to industry credit groups, you really have no idea if the customer has deteriorated. When companies get into financial difficulty, they pick and choose whom to pay. In actuality, this hypothetical customer may have been put on credit hold by every other widget manufacturer and the reason for your increase in orders is not that the customer is growing, but that no one else will sell to it.

You may think that as long as you are getting paid you should have no problem. You may even reason that since your product has high margins you can afford to not get paid for one shipment given the huge increase in orders. If this is your reasoning, you haven't taken preferences into account and we strongly suggest you read the bankruptcy chapter in this book. There is also the good possibility that the last payment this customer gives you (if it does pay) will be a check that bounces.

While some may not call what this customer is doing fraud, others think it is. In any event, this scenario should serve as notice to those who either don't perform annual credit reviews on customers with good paying habits or those who don't participate in industry credit groups. There is one final note in closing this topic. Occasionally, a customer gets into trouble and backs itself into a financial corner. Rather than deal with the issue, the customer quietly closes its doors and disappears leaving a string of creditors behind, effectively turning its situation into a bust-out. Don't be one of those creditors with unpaid invoices outstanding.

Bust-outs

One of the worst nightmares for credit professionals is to discover that they have become victims of fraud—a theoretically good customer is actually a thief and has successfully executed what is referred to as a bust-out. While there are many variations on the theme, what generally happens with a bust-out is that a crooked operator moves into town and begins to order goods from a number of vendors. The orders are generally small and payment is always prompt. Gradually, the thief gains the confidence of its suppliers. One day a large order appears accompanied by a request for extended terms.

The thief gets the goods, sells them at a bargain price, and skips town. When creditors try to collect, they find disconnected phones, abandoned space, and most importantly, no trace of the bust-out artist. The fact that a number of other concerns in town were also fooled is unlikely to appease the credit professional's boss.

How to Protect against a Bust-out

The old adage of "Know thy Customer" is a good one when it comes to guarding a company from such crooks. In its excellent pamphlet, *Fraud Alert,* Margolin, Weiner & Evans (MW& E) recommends:

- Require the prospective customer to fill out a complete disclosure form, including banking, credit, and character references

- Be vigilant in checking references. Verify any information prospective customers provide by reviewing Dun & Bradstreet reports and calling trade and credit references

- Inquire further, if a prospective customer appears suspect. The Better Business Bureau, as well as local and state law enforcement agencies, can facilitate the inquiry. If necessary or advisable, hire a certified fraud examiner to assist in conducting new customer due diligence.

Customer Disclosure Forms

Margolin, Weiner & Evans recommends that the following questions be included on the customer disclosure form:

- How long has the business existed?
- How long has the business operated in this particular area?
- Does the business have a history of moving from one location to another?
- Does the business maintain any ties to the community, such as membership in local organizations?

- Where does the business maintain its bank accounts?
- Where does the business maintain its office?
- Is the office a street address or a post office box?
- If an office exists, does the business appear to be conducted there or is it an empty storefront?
- Who is the principal owner and will he or she provide a personal financial statement?
- Will the principal owner personally guarantee the business obligations?

With responses to these questions, credit professionals will be well on their way to identifying potential scam artists. "If a prospective customer seems forthcoming and is willing to let you inquire of its references," warns MW&E, "then perhaps that customer is trustworthy. If the response is along the lines of 'we don't need these formalities, you can trust us,' avoid that customer." In addition to its accounting role, MW&E assists companies in conducting background checks on customers and in other matters relating to fraud. The company can be reached at mwe@mwellp.com.

Piercing the Corporate Veil

Often, debtors will try and hide assets under another name or in another entity. This is done to throw creditors off their tracks and frankly, as can be seen in the example above, to avoid paying bills. It is the task of the credit professionals, with assistance from a variety of sources, to uncover these situations. The legal profession calls this "piercing the corporate veil." In The Real World, "Piercing the Corporate Veil Case Study," attorney Scott Blakeley (www.vendorlaw.com) shares the details of one such case.

How One Credit Pro
Pierced the Corporate Veil to Collect on Unintentional Fraud

Because of the size of credit demanded by a smaller mid-size customer, the credit manager required quarterly financial statements from the customer's accounting firm. He noted that the company, which was 100% owned by a husband and wife, had a slowly dwindling cash position. When asked about it, the couple said it was a result of normal business conditions. Eventually, payments stopped, leaving the supplier with several hundred thousand dollars outstanding.

The account was then turned over to a collection agency. Since the vendor in question was the customer's main supplier and it had stopped shipping, the business was winding down and the agency was not able to collect. The account was then turned over to a lawyer who sued the customer. The vendor won a judgment in court but at that point there was nothing left to collect. At this point, the company was able to subpoena bank records, which showed a series of checks written to the couple and deposited in their personal accounts. They had slowly and systematically drained the assets from the company. Whether this was their intent when they started the business or not, the result was the same as a bust-out. They had siphoned off all the assets from the company.

Now a less conscientious credit manager might have written this account off to bad debt but not this one. His collection agency thought that the principles might have assets. Despite the fact that the vendor had not gotten a personal guarantee, the vendor went after the husband and wife personally in court. He was able to do this because the couple owned 100% of the company.

The paper trail led back to the company. A background search turned up personal assets. For example, a local title search uncovered the fact that the couple owned property while a lien search uncovered no mortgage. They owned their home free and clear.

The case went to trial and the couple lost. The judge began the assignment of proceeds by requiring the wife to turn over to the creditor the mink coat and diamond rings she had arrogantly worn to court. Eventually, the creditor foreclosed on the home and recovered all its money.

Piercing the Corporate Veil Case Study

Your corporate customer, a service firm that you extended a six-figure credit line to, fails to pay. You sue when other collection efforts do not result in payment. You get a money judgment, and make plans to execute on the judgment. However, in moving to execute on the assets, you discover that the officers of your corporate customer have created a new corporation and moved the assets into this new corporation.

Is the creation of the new company a legitimate business tactic or vendor fraud? Have the officers created the new company to make it judgment proof? May you collect on your judgment against the new corporation for fraud? A New Jersey Court of Appeal, in *Karo Marketing Corporation, Inc. v. Playdrome America,* recently ruled so. It found that such a vendor had claims for fraud and piercing the corporate veil when the corporation transferred assets to a newly formed company to make the original company judgment proof.

The Facts

The vendor provided advertising services to its corporate customer, a management services company, on open account. The customer failed to pay, and the vendor sued, obtaining a judgment. The debtor's primary asset was a management contract. Prior to the vendor executing on the debtor's assets to satisfy the judgment, the debtor created a new corporation and transferred the assets to the newly formed company. The new company took over the space of the company and the computers, employed the staff of the former company, and was started with a check drawn on the debtor's funds.

The vendor sued the new company for fraud, fraudulent conveyance, and piercing the corporate veil to collect on the judgment, contending that the new company was created to perform the same functions as the prior company had performed for the purpose of avoiding the judgment. The appellate court considered the fraudulent conveyance laws and piercing the corporate veil.

Writ of Attachment

Although not addressed by the court, in addition to filing a lawsuit to collect on a delinquent account, a vendor may move to attach a debtor's assets prior to a final determination of the claims sued on. The attachment creates a lien on the debtor's property to protect the vendor's priority.

Piercing the Corporate Veil

A court may disregard a corporate shield upon a showing of certain factors, including: the corporation's separate identity is not honored, a commingling of corporate funds, a failure to observe corporate formalities, and a failure to contribute capital.

Fraudulent Transfer Act

A vendor may avoid two forms of transfers by a debtor that are fraudulent as to creditors: (1) the intentional fraudulent transfer, wherein the debtor transfers assets with the intent to hinder, delay, or defraud its creditors; (2) the constructive fraudulent transfer, wherein the debtor transfers assets for less than reasonably equivalent value while it was in financial straits (such as insolvency at the time of transfer, possessing unreasonably small capital as a result of the transfer, or incurring debts beyond its ability to repay by virtue of the transfer).

IN THE REAL WORLD CONTINUED

Both the intentional and constructive fraudulent transfer provisions are part of the Uniform Fraudulent Conveyance Act or the Uniform Fraudulent Transfer Act. Each state has adopted a variant of these acts. In California, for example, under the Uniform Fraudulent Transfer Act, an intentional fraudulent transfer may be avoided up to one year after the transfer.

Creditors need not establish that the debtor was in financial straits at the time of the transfer. In California, under the Uniform Fraudulent Transfer Act, a constructive fraudulent transfer may be avoided for up to four years (and possibly seven years) after the transfer. The policy supporting the constructive fraudulent transfer is that a debtor may transfer assets for any value while it is financially healthy and paying its creditors. It is when the debtor is in financial straits and creditors will not be paid in full that the transfer may be attacked as one where the transfer did not yield fair value for the asset.

The Defense

The officers of the company contended that the new company was formed to deal with tax problems. The appellate court disagreed, applying fraud and alter ego claims.

> Here plaintiff may not have had a right to expect that [debtor] would always continue in business or that it would always have sufficient liquidity to pay its debts, but it certainly had the right to assume [debtor] would not be put out of business simply by altering legal identities and thereby rendering it insolvent for the explicit purpose of preventing plaintiff from collecting payment on its contract and subsequent judgment.

The court noted that when the debtor was about to have its assets levied, it was stripped of its assets in an attempt to defeat the vendor's judgment. The court noted that for a company to transfer all of its assets to thwart a vendor's judgment is fraud.

IN THE REAL WORLD CONTINUED

Conclusion

The *Karo Marketing* ruling reminds the credit professional holding a judgment that a crafty debtor may take extraordinary steps to avoid the judgment. Perseverance is often the key to collect on the judgment.

Escheat

Many credit professionals, their management, and their accountants think that the unclaimed property laws (also called escheat laws) do not apply to credit balances. They simply write the balance off to miscellaneous income without doing any research. They are wrong. As you will read, there are ways to research these balances so that they can either be properly written off or returned to the customer. If these procedures are followed, a company will have no credit balances to turn over to the state.

Many professionals also believe that even if they don't follow the unclaimed property regulations, they will never be caught. This is not a good assumption. As states look for ways to generate income without increasing taxes on voters, unclaimed property is a prime target. Many states have increased their audit staffs while others use third-party services. Even worse, for the companies undergoing an unclaimed property audit, some states are banding together with one auditor doing audits for several states. Surviving one audit and perhaps paying a small fine is no guarantee that the problem is over. After all, there are 50 states—and many talk to each other and cooperate on this issue.

Business-to-Business (B2B) Unclaimed Property Exception: Myth or Reality?

Unclaimed property is a topic most credit professionals would like to ignore. Unfortunately, state regulations do not permit this, and pretending the company has no escheat responsibilities could end up costing a company a lot of time, money, and aggravation. Many were hoping that credit balances would be exempted under revised rulings, but that's not exactly what happened. The following section looks at the escheat situation today.

Background

As most credit professionals are well aware, escheatment is a requirement that all unclaimed property be turned over to the state. The specifics of when and how vary from state to state. Included in the definition of *unclaimed property* are uncashed checks and credit balances—the area in which the trouble starts for most credit professionals. After the credit sits on the books for a period of time, some companies pocket the funds, writing them off to miscellaneous income. This, unfortunately, is not correct.

B2B Exception

Many in the field were counting on the much-ballyhooed business-to-business exception to take care of the problem. Readers should be aware that the states call this the vendor-to-vendor exception. It is based on the theory that outstanding balances between two business partners actually represent a duplicate payment or that the difference has been taken care of in a separate transaction. Under this explanation, companies would not have to turn the unclaimed property over to the state.

B2B Exception Today

Here's what happened. Nine states, including Maryland and Ohio, have enacted legislation enabling the B2B exception. "But," warns Karen Anderson, an Unclaimed Property Recovery & Reporting, Inc. (UPRR) vice president, "there are very few situations where it actually applies." Why? Anderson explains that the difficulties arose in the ruling of *Texas v. New Jersey.*

To put the ruling in simple terms, even if one state, in this case Texas, does not require the unclaimed property to be turned over, another state, say New Jersey, could demand, under its guidelines, that the property be turned over to it.

Anderson says that the only time a professional can feel safe in not escheating is when the transaction involves two companies in a no-escheat state and neither has responsibilities to escheat to any other state. For most readers, this ruling negates the B2B exception. If you have more detailed questions about the specifics of your company's situation, UPRR advises companies on appropriate escheat procedures.

The answer, it appears, is that the B2B exemption is more myth than reality.

IN THE REAL WORLD

How One Credit Pro
Manages the Escheat Issue

Botts has some unique views about escheatment and uses good escheat practices to enhance Meyers Printing Company's reputation among its customers. She treats all credit balances as though they were invoices. Once a credit balance is 30 days old, she contacts the customer in the same manner that she follows up with invoices that are 30 days past due. She tries to contact the customer three times over a period of 90 days. If she still has not received a response, she makes one final attempt to contact the company before stepping up her efforts.

Botts then searches on the Internet for information about the company. She also checks the credit application for the home address of the principal. It is rare that this individual does not know how to get in touch with the business owners. Finally, using the Internet, she finds a nearby company. For example, if the company had the address 815 Main Street, she'd get on the Internet and find out what business was located at 817 Main Street. Once Botts has identified the neighbor, she gets in touch with that company to see if they have any information about the whereabouts of the missing customer.

With such exhaustive investigative efforts, Meyers does not remit much to the state. To date, the company has not had to escheat any funds. It has been able to return all funds to their rightful owners. She points out that although some credit professionals suppress credit balance information from customers, eventually taking these funds into miscellaneous income, this practice is not legal nor a good business practice. Her approach is to be fair with all customers and let them know that she treats them ethically.

There are advantages to this approach. For starters, it builds goodwill with customers. Botts tells of an instance where a customer had a credit balance of over $7,000. After doing a little investigation, she was able to determine that there was a new buyer involved who did not realize the balance was available. When she informed him, rather than asking that the money be remitted to his company, he placed an order. This is an account that the company might have lost completely, as there were many new buyers in the industry that had their own suppliers that they have established relationships with. Also, by following up 30 days after the credit appears on the books instead of six months or more down the road, our chances of locating the customer are much better. Everyone's memory regarding the transactions is better as well. It is much easier and less time consuming to take care of escheat issues on an ongoing basis than to try to deal with a number of credit balances two or three years after the fact.

Alternate Dispute Resolution: Alternatives to Legal Action

A court suit can be costly, time consuming, and nerve wracking. Even if the company eventually wins its case it may not come out ahead of the game when all the costs are factored in. Thus, many companies turn to alternative dispute resolution (ADR), namely arbitration and mediation. In fact, some companies include an ADR in their sales contract. The following basic information comes from the American Arbitration Association (AAA). Those interested in the concept should visit the www.adr.org Web site for additional information.

Mediation

A meeting between disputants, their representatives, and a mediator to discuss a settlement. The mediator's role is to help the disputants explore issues, needs, and settlement options. The mediator may offer suggestions and point out issues that the disputants may have overlooked, but resolution of the dispute rests with the disputants themselves. A mediation conference can be scheduled very quickly and requires a relatively small amount of preparation time. The conference usually begins with a joint discussion of the case, followed by the mediator working with the disputants both together and separately, if appropriate, to resolve the case. Many cases are resolved within a few hours. Perhaps most important, mediation works! Statistics show that 85% of commercial matters and 95% of personal injury matters end in written settlement agreements.

Arbitration

Arbitration is referral of a dispute to one or more impartial persons for final and binding determination. Private and confidential, it is designed for quick, practical, and economical settlements. Parties can exercise

IN THE REAL WORLD

Arbitration in Action

When Paychex's credit manager, Mike Monnat, heard a talk about arbitration, he thought it was the perfect option for his company's standard contract. He has been using binding arbitration successfully for five years. Initially, he was afraid that he would never be able to convince senior management on this concept, considering that one member is an attorney, but he made a presentation right after Paychex settled a problem account that had kept the company tied up in court for three years! Binding arbitration promised to be faster and simpler, so management adopted it.

Paychex uses arbitration to help with collection disputes. It includes ADR language in its standard contract. By including it in the contract, the customer knows that Paychex takes collection issues seriously and will take the necessary steps to ensure that it gets paid. If a company refuses to sign the agreement, then Paychex does not do business with them. On a number of occasions, the company has used the arbitration process to its benefit. In the instances where the claims were smaller, Paychex has been able to have several claims heard in one day. It is far less expensive than hiring a lawyer.

Here's how the process works. When the company has a claim, it has it heard locally by an arbitrator. If the claim is won and paid, that is the end of it. If not, the claim is then turned into a judgment and enforced as any other claim would be.

Because binding arbitration is so simple and relatively inexpensive, there may be a tendency to use it too frequently. Paychex's experience has been that it can take a debtor to arbitration and win. That part is easy. Paychex has a perfect record of 100% of decisions in its favor and for the full amount. Some don't like arbitration because it has a bad reputation because it seemed like the parties were being asked to compromise and settle for a lesser amount. That has never happened to Paychex. However, it can still be very difficult and possibly cost prohibitive to collect. So, it pays to be cautious and pursue debtors who, for example, are not "judgment proof."

additional control over the arbitration process by adding specific provisions to their contracts' arbitration clauses or, when a dispute arises, through the modification of certain of the arbitration rules to suit a particular dispute. Stipulations may be made regarding confidentiality of proprietary information used; evidence, locale, number of arbitrators; and issues subject to arbitration, as examples. The parties may also provide for expedited arbitration procedures, including the time limit for rendering an award, if they anticipate a need for hearings to be scheduled on short notice. All such mutual agreements will be binding on the AAA as well as the arbitrator.

The AAA has also developed special supplementary procedures for large, complex disputes for cases where the disclosed claim of any party is at least $1,000,000.

Prior to the initial hearing in a case, the AAA may schedule either an administrative conference with the parties or a preliminary hearing with the arbitrator(s) and the parties to arrange for such matters as the production of relevant documents and the identification of witnesses, and for discussion of and agreement by the parties to any desired rule modifications. The AAA administration is guided by those decisions that the parties make as to how to handle such sensitive issues as privacy of proceedings, confidentiality, trade secrets, evidence, proprietary information, and injunctive relief.

Summary

The legal issues affecting the credit and collection function are many. By having a basic understanding of them, credit professionals are in the best position to keep their companies from violating these laws. Keep in mind that the final arbiter on legal issues should be your firm's legal counsel.

CHAPTER 10

Bankruptcy

After reading this chapter you will be able to

- Understand the differences between the different types of bankruptcy
- Fully understand your rights as a creditor
- Recognize the importance of filing proof of claims
- Recognize the implications of reclamation
- Work with preference claims against your firm

Dealing with bankrupt customers is one of the more unpleasant aspects of the credit and collection professional's job. However it must be done. Thus, a good understanding of what's involved and what can be done when a customer goes bankrupt is crucial. It is important to realize that just because you have been paid, you are not free and clear. As implausible as it may seem, under certain circumstances the bankruptcy court can and does require creditors to pay back funds received from a customer who has filed for bankruptcy protection. While some find the topic unpleasant, many others find it fascinating.

A Caveat

Like any other legal topic, bankruptcy issues can be intricate and are continually changing. What is presented here is an overview that attempts to give the reader a basic understanding of the issues related to bankruptcy from the unsecured creditor's point of view. The reader should also be aware that there has been much talk about revising the bankruptcy laws as they currently stand. There was a real chance this was going to happen in 2001 until the economy faltered and the events of September 11 happened. After that, no one had the stomach to take the hard steps needed to revise the current bankruptcy statutes.

At some point in the future, bankruptcy reform will be undertaken again. Credit professionals are advised to consult legal counsel regarding all bankruptcy issues.

Different Chapters

There are different chapters of bankruptcies under the bankruptcy code. Specifically:

- Chapter 7 is a liquidation of the business.
- Chapter 11 is a reorganization that permits the company to operate on an ongoing concern.
- Chapter 13 provides that creditors are repaid in installments in full or part over a three- to five-year period.
- Chapter 12 is designed to meet the needs of financially distressed family farmers.

Different Types of Bankruptcy

A bankruptcy can be either voluntary or involuntary. It is considered voluntary when the debtor files a petition for liquidation with the bankruptcy court. An involuntary filing occurs when:

- Three or more creditors hold a total of at least $10,000 in claims, not subject to a bona fide dispute
- There are less than 12 creditors, one creditor with at least $10,000 may file a petition

Generally speaking, the court will grant the involuntary petition if:

- The debtor is not generally paying its debts as they become due (unless such debts are subject to a bona fide dispute)
- Within 120 days prior to the filing of the petition, a custodian, other than a trustee, receiver, or agent who takes less than all of the assets of the debtor, was appointed to take charge of property of the debtor for the purpose of enforcing a lien against such property

But do not think that an involuntary filing is something to be taken lightly or that it can be used to force a debtor to do something it is not required to do. The consequences of an inappropriate filing are severe. If the court dismisses an involuntary filing, the creditor may be liable for costs, which are generally nominal and reasonable attorneys' fees for defending the involuntary petition. There can be additional assessments for any damages caused as a result of a trustee taking possession of the assets of the debtor.

When Is a Company Bankrupt?

A company is legally considered bankrupt when it is either insolvent or can no longer meet its current obligations. This is determined in one of two ways.

1. *The Balance Sheet Test.* A buyer is insolvent if its debts exceed the fair market value of its assets. This definition is covered under the Uniform Commercial Code (UCC) and is most commonly used by the bankruptcy courts as the definition to determine insolvency.

2. *The Equity Test.* A buyer is insolvent when it has ceased to pay its debts as they become due.

Brankruptcy is more difficult to prove using the balance sheet test, as a buyer may be insolvent under the equity test but not under the balance sheet test.

Creditors' Rights

All is not lost when a customer files for bankruptcy protection. Creditors do have rights. Attorney Scott Blakeley was asked about this issue, and he provided the information in the following discussion.

Commencement of Chapter 11 Case

A chapter 11 bankruptcy allows for the reorganization of the debtor-in-possession through its continuation of business. The debtor may continue to sell its goods or services while attempting to restructure itself to become a viable company. This restructuring may involve the sale or abandonment of certain assets, the rejection (cancellation) of certain contracts, and, of course, the *rescheduling* (a euphemism for stiffing its creditors) of the prepetition debts owed by the bankrupt company.

A chapter 11 bankruptcy is distinct from other types of bankruptcy filings, the most common of which are a chapter 7 bankruptcy, which provides for a trustee to gather all the nonexempt assets of the debtor and convert the assets to cash and distribute the cash to creditors, or a chapter 13 bankruptcy, which is designed for individuals who regularly earn income to pay off creditors over a set period of time.

Under chapter 11, it is presumed that the debtor will remain in possession and current management will continue to manage its affairs. Subject to bankruptcy court approval, the debtor may retain professionals to assist in its reorganization including retention of bankruptcy counsel and accountants. The bankruptcy court need not employ the debtor's officers, but a form detailing officer's compensation and experience must be filed with the U.S. Trustee and served on the committee of unsecured creditors.

The Debtor Is Treated as a Separate Entity

The prepetition debtor is treated as a separate entity from the postpetition debtor-in-possession. Therefore, contracts and documents that the prepetition debtor signed (e.g., dealer agreements, security agreements, consignment agreements, etc.) may not be enforceable against the debtor.

The vendor should distinguish between the entity before bankruptcy and after bankruptcy by drawing a demarcation between obligations and payments, which were incurred or received prior to and those incurred or received after the filing of the bankruptcy. The vendor should treat the debtor as a new and separate account for legal, accounting, and billing purposes.

Operating the Debtor

After the bankruptcy filing, the debtor operates in bankruptcy (however, the debtor can be replaced by a trustee upon a showing of bad acts by the debtor). Other than cash or cash equivalents, the debtor is permitted to use, sell, or lease property of the estate in the ordinary course of its business without court intervention. What is the ordinary course of a debtor's business has been defined by courts as those transactions that are commonly undertaken by companies in the debtor's industry. Where a transaction is out of the ordinary course of a debtor's business, and no court order is obtained, the transaction is an impermissible postpetition transfer subject to avoidance.

The debtor generally will be a party to executory contracts, including license agreements, distribution agreements, collective bargaining agreements, stock repurchase agreements, and conditional sales agreements at the time of its filing.

Leases

With commercial real estate leases, a debtor has 60 days from the date of the bankruptcy filing to assume, assume and assign, reject, or, for cause, extend the period to assume or reject. With all other executory contracts or unexpired leases, a debtor must elect to assume or reject at the time the plan is confirmed.

Sufficient grounds for assumption or rejection are that either assumption or rejection is consistent with the exercise of the debtor's business judgment. To assume an executory contract or unexpired lease in default, a debtor must satisfy a dual obligation before a court will allow assumption: It must cure and assure. To cure, a debtor must pay all prepetition arrearages. To assure, a debtor must make a showing that it is capable of performing the assumed lease.

The Bankruptcy Code permits the debtor to sell assets outside the ordinary course of business, subject to court approval. The Bankruptcy Code permits the debtor to sell assets free and clear of liens, with the proceeds put in an account for distribution to the lien holders.

Automatic Stay Protects the Debtor

Upon the filing of the bankruptcy petition, an injunction automatically goes into effect. The injunction, or automatic stay, is very broad and enjoins any creditor or party from taking any action against property of the estate without first obtaining relief from stay. In a chapter 11 proceeding, the automatic stay is in effect until confirmation of the plan.

The debtor's bankruptcy "stays" the creditors from collecting any prepetition debt owed by the debtor to the creditors of the debtor. A creditor who is secured may seek *relief from the automatic stay* to recover its collateral if the debtor cannot provide *adequate protection* for the creditor.

Notice of Commencement of Case and Meeting of Creditors

All creditors in the case scheduled by the debtor receive a notice of commencement. The U.S. Trustee sets a Final Meeting of Creditors date, which is included with the notice of commencement. The First Meeting of Creditors is held 20 to 40 days after the bankruptcy filing.

At this meeting, the debtor's officers and attorney will made a brief presentation as to the cause for the bankruptcy filing and what steps it is taking, and intends to take, to pay creditors and exit bankruptcy. Creditors are allowed to ask question of the debtor at this meeting. The first meeting of creditors is commonly referred to as the 341 meeting—named after a section of the bankruptcy code.

Appointment of Creditors Committee

Once appointed, the committee then holds a meeting and appoints counsel to represent it. The committee may investigate the debtor and monitor the operation of the business. The committee may also play a substantial role in the development of the plan of reorganization. As a party in the proceeding, the committee is entitled to be served with all pleadings filed by the debtor with the bankruptcy court, and as a significant party in interest, the committee may instruct its counsel to object to any pleadings the debtor files which are inconsistent with the committee's goals.

Claims Process

In order to establish their rights, creditors must file a proof of claim, which the debtor may object to. Specifically:

- *Proof of claim.* Creditors scheduled by the debtor as holding contingent, disputed, or unliquidated claims must file a proof of claim with the bankruptcy court within a time fixed by the court. This is achieved by filing a proof of claim supported by documentation supporting that claim by the date set by the court. The steps needed to file such a claim are delineated under "Timing of Proof of Claim," later in this chapter.

- *Objection to claims.* Parties in interest may file objections to claims of creditors from which the court will hold a hearing to determine the validity of the claim.

Cash Collateral

A debtor makes a motion to use cash collateral that is held as security by a secured party. The court will hear the motion on cash collateral and determine the debtor's right to use it by analyzing the amount of security available to the creditor and the debt outstanding.

Liquidation of the Debtor's Assets

The Bankruptcy Code allows for the sale of substantially all of the assets of the debtor, upon approval of the bankruptcy court. Generally, a major asset sale eliminates the need for a plan that provides for the debtor's reorganization; rather a liquidation plan will be filed. A sale can occur at any stage of the bankruptcy proceeding, but is most common at the early stages of the case.

Chapter 11 Plan

The goal of a chapter 11 plan is to allow the debtor to recognize and operate in a hopefully profitable manner in the future. Steps include the following:

1. *Debtor's exclusive right to file plan.* The debtor has the exclusive right to file a plan of reorganization during the first 120 days from the filing of the petition, plus any extension that may be granted by the court.

2. *Plan of reorganization.* A plan of reorganization and disclosure statement must be filed with the court. The creditors committee or the debtor may draft the plan or a consensual plan may be drafted between both the committee and the debtor. The plan of reorganization is, in essence, an agreement between the debtor and its creditors that provide for rewriting the prefiling obligations of the debtor, and classifies claims and interests of creditors and specifies their treatment under the plan.

3. *Confirmation of the plan.* Creditors who are impaired under the plan vote on the plan. The court will enter an order confirming the plan and move toward consummation of the plan. Hearings regarding objections to claims are ongoing during the consummation of the plan. Once a final determination is made as to all administrative matters and costs, the plan is then implemented.

4. *Final decree.* After the estate is fully administered, the court enters a final decree closing the case. Unlike chapter 11 proceedings, which provide for reorganization (or, in certain circumstances, a liquidating plan of reorganization), a chapter 7 filing provides for a liquidation of a debtor's assets. Individuals, partnerships, and corporations are eligible chapter 7 debtors; however, as corporations are not entitled to a discharge, corporations instead may seek liquidation under state law.

Upon the chapter 7 filing, a bankruptcy estate is created wherein all property in which the debtor has an interest at the time of the bankruptcy filing, and certain contingent assets—such as an inheritance or proceeds from a life insurance policy—up to six months after the bankruptcy filing, are included. With the bankruptcy filing, the debtor obtains the benefit of the automatic stay, which enjoins vendors from taking action to collect their debts. As a chapter 7 acts as a snapshot in time, an individual's earnings post–bankruptcy filing are not included in the chapter 7 estate.

Chapter 7

Unlike chapter 11, which provides for the appointment of a trustee only upon a showing of compelling facts, a chapter 7 proceeding provides for the automatic appointment of a trustee in every case. The primary purpose of an individual filing under chapter 7 is to obtain a discharge of prefiling obligations, the so-called "fresh start," to which an honest debtor is entitled. To facilitate the fresh start of the debtor, a chapter 7 bankruptcy is designed to move promptly to a discharge of the debtor's prefiling obligations, usually within six months. The following significant events make up the cycle of the chapter 7 proceeding:

- Simultaneously with the chapter 7 filing, an interim trustee is selected from a panel of trustees by the office of the U.S. Trustee to administer the debtor's assets. The U.S. Trustee, an adjunct of the Justice Department, has responsibility for overseeing the administration of bankruptcy cases. The interim trustee serves as the permanent trustee unless there is vendor opposition. The debtor is required to file schedules that describe in detail its assets and liabilities with a list of vendors within 15 days of the bankruptcy filing. The debtor is permitted to select a schedule of exemptions under either state law or the Bankruptcy Code, which provides certain assets to be excluded from the bankruptcy estate for the debtor's benefit.

- The schedule of exemptions also must be filed within 15 days of the chapter 7 filing. Examples of such exemptions include exemptions for individual retirement account (IRA) and Employment Retirement Income Security Act (ERISA) profit-sharing plans. Within 20 to 40 days of the bankruptcy filing, the interim trustee convenes a section 341 meeting or *first meeting of vendors.*

- All vendors scheduled by the debtor are given notice of the meeting by the bankruptcy court and are invited to attend. At the section 341 meeting, the trustee will question the debtor briefly as to its assets, liabilities, and financial affairs. Vendors are also given an opportunity to briefly question the debtor. The total time for questioning the debtor by the trustee and vendors is generally but a few minutes. Should the section 341 meeting prove uneventful, the trustee will issue its no-asset report, signifying the debtor has no assets, and that there will be no distribution to unsecured vendors. Unlike chapter 11, there is no vendors' committee formed in a chapter 7 bankruptcy. Rather, vendors are to work together informally and through the trustee.

- Upon appointment, the trustee gathers and takes control of property of the estate, including prosecution of lawsuits. The trustee abandons property it deems burdensome or of inconsequential value. The trustee moves to sell the assets collected upon notice to all vendors and pursuant to bankruptcy court order. Auctions to the public are common.

- Unless the court sustains an objection to discharge, the debtor obtains a discharge of its prefiling, unsecured obligations. Vendors holding secured claims will have their unsecured claims for any deficiency judgments against the individual debtor discharged, but are entitled to their collateral.

- Where the interim trustee determines a distribution to unsecured vendors is anticipated, a bar date is set, which requires vendors to file proofs of claim no later than 90 days after the notice to all vendors is mailed by the bankruptcy court. The trustee reconciles the claims and files objections where necessary.

- In chapter 7, there is no plan filed. Rather, the trustee files with the bankruptcy court its final account, which shows the cash on hand and the proposed distribution. The bankruptcy court must order the distribution, based on the priority scheme provided under the Bankruptcy Code. Thereafter, the court will close the estate.

The Bankruptcy Code grants the trustee authority over all of the debtor's assets. The trustee is vested with the primary responsibility to undertake an immediate investigation into the debtor's assets and liabilities, including uncovering any mismanagement or misconduct, which might have led to the bankruptcy filing.

Trustee Obligations in a Chapter 7 proceeding

The trustee is obligated to undertake certain steps to ensure the maximum payout for creditors. These include the following:

- The trustee also has the obligation to institute litigation whenever necessary to collect assets of the estate. It is not for the vendors themselves, but rather the trustee, to pursue causes of action on behalf of the estate.

- The trustee has the duty to oppose the debtor's discharge when necessary and provide information to parties in interest. Trustees must use reasonable care in carrying out their duties.

While the Bankruptcy Code clearly provides the trustee with broad powers to collect assets of the estate, including prosecution of lawsuits, there is a fundamental conflict facing trustees: On the one hand, trustees are expected to handle cases more efficiently and to conclude cases more quickly, while on the other hand trustees are still burdened with a crushing caseload that does not permit them to devote time to properly investigate each case.

Who Are Trustees?

Trustees are not employees of the government. Rather, they are attorneys, accountants, or businesspeople who are compensated as trustees by receiving a flat fee of $45 for each no-asset chapter 7 case they conclude, and, in asset chapter 7 cases with a distribution to vendors, a percentage of all money disbursed for each estate. Trustees concede the compensation structure does not provide an incentive to pursue assets where a substantial investigation is required and recovery is speculative, as they take these types of cases essentially on a contingency. Thus, to attract the trustee to pursue assets in a so-called no-asset chapter 7, vendors must fund the trustee's recovery efforts.

What Can Credit Pros Do?

Fortunately, there is action vendors may take on their own without the need to hire professionals to determine whether the debtor has concealed or disposed of assets. However, before commencing an investigation, vendors should first consider any claims or causes of action available against the debtor and third parties under the Bankruptcy Code:

- *Object.* The vendors' investigation will be guided by the claims they are seeking to develop. The most common claims or causes of action include objections to exemptions and objections to a debtor's discharge. An objection to exemptions deals with whether the debtor has undervalued exempted assets or designated assets for exemption that are improper.

    Objection to a debtor's discharge are based on several grounds including:

    - The debtor transferred, concealed, or destroyed property within one year before the bankruptcy filing or any time after the filing
    - The debtor concealed, destroyed, or failed to keep books and records
    - The debtor made a false oath or withheld information from an officer of the estate
    - The debtor is unable to explain loss of his property
    - The debtor has received a discharge in a prior bankruptcy within six years

- The debtor has had a discharge waived or denied in a prior bankruptcy case

Many of the grounds for objecting to a discharge may also constitute federal crimes. Vendors may also seek to have their particular debt to be ordered nondischargeable. The most common causes of action to exclude particular debts from discharge are:

- Fraudulently incurred obligations

- Fiduciary fraud and embezzlement

- Willful and malicious acts

- *Preferences.* Vendors should also determine whether the estate holds any preference or fraudulent conveyance claims. Under a preference theory, certain transfers made by the debtor 90 days prior to the bankruptcy filing date (one year for insiders) and while the debtor was insolvent may be brought back into the estate, subject to certain defenses.

  Under a theory of constructive fraudulent conveyance, certain transfers made by the debtor, up to four years prior to the bankruptcy filing in California, may be avoidable where it can be established that the debtor did not receive reasonably equivalent value in the transaction.

  Under a theory of intentional fraudulent conveyance, prepetition transfers made by the debtor with the intent to hinder, delay, or defraud vendors may be avoided.

- *Review.* The first step in the vendor's investigation to establish the respective claims is to review the debtor's bankruptcy schedules and statement of financial affairs. Vendors should compare the information contained in the bankruptcy schedules with any financial statements the debtor recently prepared to determine whether any significant assets may have been omitted from the bankruptcy petition or whether the debtor assigned dramatically different values to the assets.

Debtors are required to disclose in their bankruptcy schedules any assets that were transferred outside the ordinary course of the debtor's financial dealings one year prior to the filing. Vendors should also review the bankruptcy schedules to confirm the assets the debtor is seeking to exempt from the estate and verify the values the debtor has assigned to those assets. Vendors should start this investigation as soon as possible after the bankruptcy filing so that they may intelligently question the debtor at the section 341 meeting. Alternatively, vendors may provide to the trustee the information obtained from such investigation for the trustee's questioning of the debtor, the result of which may be a refusal by the trustee to issue a no-asset report and objection to the debtor's discharge.

- *Investigate.* What is the vendor's next step where review of the debtor's bankruptcy schedules and financial statements fails to yield answers of apparently missing assets, but suspicion of misconduct persists? Vendors should turn first to the trustee. While the trustee will likely decline requests to pursue investigation in these supposed no-asset cases, the trustee may have new information about the debtor or may offer suggestions to employ other investigatory strategies.

Adequate Attempts to Recover Assets

After consultation with the trustee, vendors must decide whether they are willing to spend "fresh" money to retain professionals to attempt to recover assets. This analysis requires a balancing of the value of the assets sought to be recovered (if known), after liquidation, with the estimated costs to locate and recover the assets. The difficulty with the analysis is determining "how deep the bodies are buried," for example, how well has the debtor hidden the assets. It may be that the costs to locate, recover, and liquidate the assets exceed the recovery itself. Perhaps money is best spent at this stage of the investigation by employing a private investigator.

A more thorough investigation may necessitate the retention of accountants to analyze the debtor's financial statements or reconstruct the disposition of assets. Vendors may also consider taking a Rule 2004 examination of the debtor. This examination, conducted by an attorney, permits broad questioning into the debtor's financial affairs. If the vendor's initial investigation identifies either tangible or intangible assets, vendors will need to take action to collect the proceeds, which often requires retention of counsel.

The Need to Move Quickly in Chapter 7

As a chapter 7 proceeding is designed to move promptly toward conclusion within six months, if it is a no-asset proceeding, vendors must likewise investigate promptly to preserve their rights to object to various aspects of the bankruptcy proceeding. Where vendors have performed their due diligence, and claims have been revealed against the debtor, the following are critical time periods for vendors to act in chapter 7.

If the debtor has improperly scheduled exemptions, objections must be filed within 30 days after the first scheduled section 341 meeting. Property is exempt where the debtor schedules the exemption and there is no objection. To object to a debtor's discharge, a complaint must be filed within 60 days after the first scheduled section 341 meeting; seeking to have a particular debt ordered nondischargeable also requires a complaint be filed within 60 days of the section 341 meeting.

The estate may also hold claims against the debtor for preference or fraudulent conveyance actions, which must be commenced within two years of the bankruptcy filing or the time the case is closed or dismissed with preference and fraudulent claims. As the trustee is the party recognized under the Bankruptcy Code with standing to pursue such lawsuits, vendors may request that counsel they had retained be employed by the trustee to sue.

Resource for Credit Professionals

Mr. Blakeley's firm has a Web site (www.vendorlaw.com) that provides credit professionals with relevant information. He also prepares a quarterly e-mail newsletter about relevant bankruptcy and creditors' rights topics. If you would like to be added to the mailing list, send an e-mail to sblakeley@vendorlaw.com giving him the relevant contact information to add your name to the e-mail distribution.

Order of Payouts

Rarely does everyone get paid out completely in a bankruptcy. Secured creditors receive 100% of their claims before any other creditor is paid. After the secured creditors are paid out, the priority of claims is as follows:

1. Claims for goods delivered to the debtor on an unsecured basis postpetition
2. Wages under $4,000
3. Commissions under $4,000
4. Severance pay under $4,000
5. Sick leave pay earned immediately prior to the bankruptcy under $4,000
6. Contributions to an employee benefit plan under $4,000
7. Certain claims of farmers for grain stored or fish delivered to a processing facility

8. Certain consumer deposits

9. Tax claims

10. Unsecured creditors

11. Stockholders

As can easily be seen, unsecured creditors generally don't fare well. That is why it is imperative that anything that can be done to improve one's standings be done and done expediently. This includes filing proof of claims and reclamation claims.

Proof of Claim

In a chapter 7 bankruptcy, a creditor must file a proof of claim in order to receive a distribution from the estate. All proof of claims must be filed within 90 days after the first date set for the 341 meeting. Credit professionals should note that the deadline is calculated from the original date of the 341 meeting and will not be extended if the 341 meeting is continued.

Credit professionals should note that the filing of a proof of claim has been held to waive a creditor's right to a jury trial on certain preference and fraudulent transfer actions, and is generally considered to be sufficient to submit the creditor to the jurisdiction of the bankruptcy court for other purposes. Therefore, unless you are satisfied that the debtor has no potential for fraudulent or preferential transfer or otherwise against you, you should discuss the filing of a claim with counsel.

Reclamation

Reclamation is the right of a seller to recover possession of goods delivered to an insolvent buyer. Sellers have the right to *reclaim* their goods from bankrupt customers in certain instances. Reclamation rights are needed when an unsecured vendor is unable to retrieve goods or stop them in transit.

Courts have settled on the following elements to establish a valid reclamation claim under the Bankruptcy code:

- The seller sold goods on credit to the debtor in the ordinary course of business of both.

- The seller delivered the goods to the debtor at a time when the debtor was insolvent.

- The seller made a written demand for the return of the goods within ten days after the goods were delivered to the debtor.

- The debtor had possession of the goods at the time of the reclamation demand or the goods were not in the hands of a buyer in the ordinary course or a good-faith purchaser at the time of demand.

Filing a reclamation claim is imperative as it could upgrade an unsecured creditor's claim to the administrative class. Alternatively, the customer could return the goods. This moves the claim up in priority and gives the creditor a real shot at getting most, if not all, of its money back. To make a successful reclamation claim:

- The vendor initiates reclamation by delivering a reclamation letter within ten days after the goods were delivered.

- The reclamation letter should include:

  - A detailed description of the merchandise in question

  - A statement of the delivery date to the debtor

  - A demand for the immediate return of the goods

- The vendor should demand an accounting of the goods sold. (*Note:* An accounting is crucial because the right to reclaim may be defeated by the debtor's resale of the goods to a buyer in the ordinary course of business.)

- If accounting is not delivered or is inaccurate, the vendor should be prepared to immediately demand a right to inspect both the inventory on hand and the books and records pertaining to sales of said goods for the period between the date of delivery of the goods and the date of the reclamation letter.

- The letter should be delivered to the debtor by fax copy *and* certified mail.

- If the buyer files bankruptcy prior to the preparation of the reclamation letter (or at any time thereafter), the vendor should promptly contact debtor's counsel in order to stipulate with debtor either to the immediate return of the goods or for the debtor to sell the goods, provided that the vendor is granted an administrative claim or a lien under the Bankruptcy Code.

- A vendor should proceed with an adversary action through the bankruptcy court to enforce its rights so as to meet its burden of proof that the goods subject to the reclamation demand were in the possession of the debtor at the time such demand was made.

Timing of Proof of Claim

Federal rule of the Bankruptcy Procedure Rules grant the Bankruptcy Court the authority to establish a deadline. In some districts, it is customary for the deadline to be established immediately upon the filing of the petition. In other districts, the court will establish and separately notice any deadline. You should review all notices.

The official Proof of Claim Form (see Exhibit 10.1) should include:

- Identity of the Bankruptcy Court (i.e., U.S. Bankruptcy Court, District of Kansas, Southern District of New York, etc.)

- Name of the debtor and either a Social Security number or tax identification number if the court lists it on its notices

- Bankruptcy case number, which will be set in the notice that you receive

- Creditor information including:
  - *Full legal name and address,* which should be a street address not a lockbox address
  - *The loan credit card or other identifying number* or put none if none exists
  - *First box to right of Name & Address.* Are you aware of anyone else filing a proof of claim relating to your claim? If checked, you must provide a copy of the claim relating to this claim.
  - *Second box to the right of Name & Address.* Did you receive a notice from the Bankruptcy Court (i.e., Did you file the claim after informally learning of the case from the newspaper, if so check the second box)?
  - *Third box to the right of the Name & Address.* This box should be checked if the address you provide to the left is in any way different from the address contained in the notice sent to you from the court.
  - *Last two boxes to the right of the Name & Address.* These boxes ensure that you are properly listed on the case mailing matrix so that you receive all subsequent notices.
  - *Final portion* asks you to indicate whether this particular claim is an amendment or replacement of a claim you previously filed.
- *Claim information.* The following sections must be addressed:
  - *Section 1.* Asks you to indicate the basis for your claim: Goods sold, services performed, money loaned, personal injury/wrongful death, taxes, retiree benefits, wages, salary, and compensation, or other—describe the legal basis for your claim.

EXHIBIT 10.1

Form B10: Proof of Claim Form

FORM B10 (Official Form 10) (4/01)

UNITED STATES BANKRUPTCY COURT _____ DISTRICT OF _____		PROOF OF CLAIM
Name of Debtor	Case Number	

NOTE: This form should not be used to make a claim for an administrative expense arising after the commencement of the case. A "request" for payment of an administrative expense may be filed pursuant to 11 U.S.C. § 503.

Name of Creditor (The person or other entity to whom the debtor owes money or property):	☐ Check box if you are aware that anyone else has filed a proof of claim relating to your claim. Attach copy of statement giving particulars.	
Name and address where notices should be sent:	☐ Check box if you have never received any notices from the bankruptcy court in this case. ☐ Check box if the address differs from the address on the envelope sent to you by the court.	
Telephone number:		THIS SPACE IS FOR COURT USE ONLY

Account or other number by which creditor identifies debtor:	Check here ☐ replaces if this claim ☐ amends a previously filed claim, dated:_____

1. Basis for Claim
- ☐ Goods sold
- ☐ Services performed
- ☐ Money loaned
- ☐ Personal injury/wrongful death
- ☐ Taxes
- ☐ Other _____

☐ Retiree benefits as defined in 11 U.S.C. § 1114(a)
☐ Wages, salaries, and compensation (fill out below)

Your SS #: _____ _____ _____

Unpaid compensation for services performed

from _____ to _____
    (date)   (date)

2. Date debt was incurred:	**3. If court judgment, date obtained:**

4. Total Amount of Claim at Time Case Filed: $ _____

If all or part of your claim is secured or entitled to priority, also complete Item 5 or 6 below.

☐ Check this box if claim includes interest or other charges in addition to the principal amount of the claim. Attach itemized statement of all interest or additional charges.

5. Secured Claim.

☐ Check this box if your claim is secured by collateral (including a right of setoff).

Brief Description of Collateral:
☐ Real Estate ☐ Motor Vehicle
☐ Other_____

Value of Collateral: $_____

Amount of arrearage and other charges at time case filed included in secured claim, if any: $_____

6. Unsecured Priority Claim.

☐ Check this box if you have an unsecured priority claim

Amount entitled to priority $_____

Specify the priority of the claim:
- ☐ Wages, salaries, or commissions (up to $4,650),* earned within 90 days before filing of the bankruptcy petition or cessation of the debtor's business, whichever is earlier - 11 U.S.C. § 507(a)(3).
- ☐ Contributions to an employee benefit plan - 11 U.S.C. § 507(a)(4).
- ☐ Up to $2,100* of deposits toward purchase, lease, or rental of property or services for personal, family, or household use - 11 U.S.C. § 507(a)(6).
- ☐ Alimony, maintenance, or support owed to a spouse, former spouse, or child - 11 U.S.C. § 507(a)(7).
- ☐ Taxes or penalties owed to governmental units - 11 U.S.C. § 507(a)(8).
- ☐ Other - Specify applicable paragraph of 11 U.S.C. § 507(a)(___).

*Amounts are subject to adjustment on 4/1/04 and every 3 years thereafter with respect to cases commenced on or after the date of adjustment.

7. Credits: The amount of all payments on this claim has been credited and deducted for the purpose of making this proof of claim.

8. Supporting Documents: *Attach copies of supporting documents,* such as promissory notes, purchase orders, invoices, itemized statements of running accounts, contracts, court judgments, mortgages, security agreements, and evidence of perfection of lien. DO NOT SEND ORIGINAL DOCUMENTS. If the documents are not available, explain. If the documents are voluminous, attach a summary.

9. Date-Stamped Copy: To receive an acknowledgment of the filing of your claim, enclose a stamped, self-addressed envelope and copy of this proof of claim.

THIS SPACE IS FOR COURT USE ONLY

Date	Sign and print the name and title, if any, of the creditor or other person authorized to file this claim (attach copy of power of attorney, if any):

Penalty for presenting fraudulent claim: Fine of up to $500,000 or imprisonment for up to 5 years, or both. 18 U.S.C. §§ 152 and 3571.

- *Section 2.* Asks you to indicate the date the debt was incurred.

- *Section 3.* If your claim is based on a court judgment, you need to provide the date the judgment was entered.

- *Section 4.* You must classify your claim: secured, unsecured priority, or unsecured nonpriority.

- *Section 5.* Asks you to set forth the unsecured, secured, and priority portions of your claim and to total these numbers to reflect the full amount of your claim.

- *Certification.* At the bottom of the claim, you must sign your name, give your title along with the date of signature, and provide a power of attorney if you are signing under one.

- *Documentation.* It is imperative to send copies of all supporting documentation to the proof of claim.

- *Copies.* Many courts require that you send two copies of your proof of claim. For your protection, a third copy should also be sent to be date and time stamped and returned to you in a self-addressed, stamped envelope for your files to use as proof that your claim was properly filed with the Clerk of the Court.

Small Claims

Some credit professionals think it is not worth their time and effort to file proofs of claim for small dollar amounts, say under $1,000. Their reasoning is that by the time the unsecured claims are paid out, say at seven cents on the dollar (the average payout on all bankruptcies), their time and efforts would be better spent elsewhere. In theory, they are correct.

However, in actuality, this reasoning may be faulty. Here's why. In many large bankruptcies where there are assets, small unsecured creditors are lumped together into an "administrative convenience class" of creditors and paid in full—just to get rid of them. Thus, before deciding not to bother with a proof of claim, credit professionals are advised to determine if there are assets in the case. If so, the time and effort preparing the claim may be well worth the while.

Creditors Committee

In any bankruptcy action, unsecured creditors need to be represented. Having all creditors at all meetings would quickly get out of hand. Thus, a representative group is typically selected. Representatives are selected from the list of trade debtors, and the top 20 balances outstanding at the time of filing are contacted by the U.S. Trustee's Office and requested to attend a meeting of debtors for the selection of a committee.

Typically, a minimum of seven creditors is selected to be on the committee (may be a maximum of 11, but always an odd number to prevent a hung jury). Credit professionals should realize that when asked to join a committee it is strictly voluntary, but there are requirements made of those that commit to joining such as:

- Accepting a fiduciary responsibility to act in the best interest not of your firm but the trade creditors in total

- Possibly approving actions which could be in direct conflict with your firm's present situation with the debtor-in-possession (i.e., supporting a motion to go after preference payments)

- Keeping confidential information provided to the committee that could help give your firm an advantage over the debtor-in-possession or put your firm at a disadvantage

- Committing the time necessary to meet the requirements of the committee (i.e., forming subcommittees that will monitor certain actions by the debtor-in-possession to prevent the disbursal or fraudulent transfer of assets out of the debtor's firm, monitoring certain financial records, or possibly offering suggestions that will aid the debtor-in-possession in improving its financial position)

When a minimum of seven creditors have agreed to participate in the committee, the representative from the U.S. Trustee's Office will officially announce that a committee has been formed and will list who their member firms are. Other firms that may wish to be considered must submit a formal request with the U.S. Trustee and if necessary with the Bankruptcy Court stating why they should be added to this group. (Once the Committee has been formed, it is very difficult to be added to it, but a firm may be added as an alternate or as a nonvoting member.)

At this point, the Committee's responsibility will be to obtain the best possible plan of reorganization, which will yield the highest payout to all unsecured trade creditors. They will become the trade creditor's "watchdog" and will finally submit a plan of reorganization if the debtor-in-possession does not come up with an approved plan. They can also petition the court to install a trustee to replace the management team currently running the firm or request that an examiner be hired to determine if the debtor-in-possession is mismanaging or fraudulently transferring assets.

The bankruptcy estate pays reasonable expenses of the Creditor's Committee as an administrative expense. They may also hire an attorney firm to represent them in any action against the estate as well as an accounting firm that will analyze the data provided by the debtor-in-possession. These expenses are also passed on to the estate.

Cram-down

From time to time credit professionals will hear reference in bankruptcy to cram-downs. This is the process by which a plan is confirmed over the objections of creditors or shareholders to the provisions of the plan. Unless the plan provides for full payment of all unsecured claims with interest over a relatively short period of time, a cram-down is going to

Cram-downs

A number of well-know bankruptcies have resulted from the debtor being unable to pay the high interest rate on its junk bonds. Once in bankruptcy, the debtor-in-possession will go to the unsecured creditors and propose to them a reorganization plan that includes:

- The unsecured creditors being paid out in full plus interest
- The interest rate on the junk bonds being drastically lowered or the debt position being converted to an equity stake

Since only one class of creditors must approve reorganization plans, most unsecured creditors offered such an option are happy to approve.

be rarely possible over the objections of unsecured creditors. The key to the success of a cram-down is the pitting of one class of creditors against another.

Certified Expert Witness Program

Recognizing that credit professionals themselves are probably the best situated to develop a defense against preference claims, the National Association of Credit Management (NACM) established a special certification in 1996. The purpose of this program is to train and certify credit professionals to judge the validity of preference claims and to testify to that appropriateness in court. Obviously, these certified individuals can also build preference defenses. In order to qualify for this rigorous program, the credit professional must have already been certified by NACM as a certified credit executive (CCE), its highest professional designation. The first time the program was run, well over 100 individuals were certified.

We turned to one such individual, Hal Schaeffer, for the following information related to preferences. He is president of D&H Credit Services Inc., and the husband of the author.

Preferences

One of the tenets of bankruptcy is that all creditors in the same class are to be treated in the same manner. One cannot be given preference over another. From this principle arises the preference issue—something few outside the bankruptcy world can fathom. Those creditors that received payments when others did not are deemed to have received a preferential transfer, and under certain circumstances are required to return those amounts.

What Is a Preferential Transfer?

A preferential transfer of the debtor's assets (either cash or merchandise) is deemed to include:

- Every mode of disposing of property whether direct or indirect, absolute or conditional, or voluntary or involuntary
- Virtually any payment, gift, or other transfer of assets may fall within the provisions, including any voluntary payment by the debtor of an outstanding unsecured bill or the satisfaction of the same debt through the seizure of assets

The transfer must go to the creditor or somehow directly benefit the creditor; be for or on account of an antecedent debt (a debt made before the filing of a bankruptcy petition).

What Is Antecedent Debt?

An antecedent debt is one that was in existence prior to the alleged preferential payment. The giving of the collateral or the repayment of the loan or trade balance, which was initially to be an unsecured loan or trade balance, constitutes payment on an antecedent debt, which may

A Classic Preference Situation

When a company begins to experience financial difficulties, it may stop paying all suppliers with the exception of one or two. The reason for this is simple: It wants these few creditors to continue supplying goods. Inevitably, the customer files for bankruptcy protection and the bankruptcy court demands that the *preferential* creditors return the funds paid within the preference period.

The first time this happens to a creditor it is likely to be outraged. Usually, by the time of the filing, the debtor will owe the creditor some money. So, in addition to the money owed (and likely to be largely unpaid) the creditor is now asked to return some of the funds it had previously received.

be deemed preferential. This may be especially true when there was a personal guarantee provided by the largest shareholder of a firm when the debt was initially made.

- While the debtor was insolvent:
  - The bankruptcy code creates a rebuttable presumption that the debtor was insolvent for the 90 calendar days preceding the filing of bankruptcy.
  - Proving this may be extremely difficult since the debtor's records are often so incoherent that it is difficult to determine the debtor's financial condition immediately preceding bankruptcy.
  - The proof required would be to show that prior to the filing date the debtor had more assets than liabilities (the balance sheet test).
- Within 90 days of the petition for relief (the period is up to one year if the transfer is to an insider): One concern that has

been tested in court has been the date that a check is tendered in the debtor's bank. This is the start date for the 90-day window, not the date of the check or the date that it is deposited in your lockbox.

- The effect of which is to give the creditor more than the creditor would otherwise receive in a chapter 7 liquidation.

  - Payments of proceeds from the liquidation of collateral subject to a properly perfected security interest are generally not preferential since the creditor would receive as much in a chapter 7 liquidation.

  - In calculating the preferential effect, the potential dividend from the bankruptcy estate as a percentage of claims is compared to a percent of the claim actually received by the transferee.

- A preference action against a creditor can be deemed to be the ultimate insult. An effective job is done in collecting the debt and then the creditor is sued to recover these payments.

- If you are dealing with a subsidiary and receive payment directly from the parent corporation, the trustee of the subsidiary will generally not be able to recover that payment from you.

Defenses to a Preference Action

Receiving a preference notice is not the end of the world. Just because a trustee has initiated a preference action against a creditor does not mean that the creditor should honor that request—just the opposite. For starters, more than one trustee has been known to simply take a debtor's checkbook and initiate preference claims for every check written in the 90 days prior to the bankruptcy filing. These trustees do no work to verify that the amount was a preference. Most bankruptcy specialists recommend that creditors do nothing when first hit with a preference action—except perhaps get their documentation together.

There are defenses against preference actions. These include:

- *Contemporaneous exchange.* This is a simultaneous transfer of funds to a creditor at the same time that the goods are delivered. The simplest example is known as cash on delivery (COD). Credit professionals should be aware that if a check from the debtor is returned twice and is then replaced with certified funds, the replacement funds are not considered COD but two separate transactions.

- *New value.* This is the payment on an old debt in exchange for new goods or services. The payment must be made before the release of new goods or services and must be a related transaction.

- *Ordinary course of business.* The transfer was in payment of a debt incurred by the debtor in the ordinary course of its business or financial affairs and of the transferee's business and financial affairs. The transfer itself was made in the ordinary course of business of both debtor and creditor when the transfer was made according to ordinary course of business terms.

Proving a Payment Was Not Preferential

It is usually left to the creditor to prove that the payment was not preferential rather than to the trustee to prove it is. The trustee is likely to provide some documentation, but the credit professional will need to prepare a defense based on the three defenses delineated above.

Out-of-Court Settlements

A popular alternative to the costly, contentious, and lengthy formal bankruptcy procedures administered by the U.S. Bankruptcy Court is a process commonly referred to as out-of-court settlements. It can be used instead of chapter 7 liquidations or chapter 11 restructuring. Because of the streamlined process, creditors receive their payouts much faster than in the traditional bankruptcy process.

Costs

Credit professionals should be aware that there are still costs associated with this type of transaction. Lawyers are hired to negotiate with the debtor and structure the transaction properly. Accountants are generally needed to value the assets and the potential payout to the unsecured debtors for their prepetition debt.

Appropriateness

Out-of-court settlements are used more frequently in certain industries, when a large percentage of the debt is held by a small number of creditors, and when there are a limited number of landlords involved, especially if rent has not been paid.

What to Require of the Debtor

For starters, the debtor should reveal the extent of its financial problems. It should also make a complete disclosure of its assets and cash on hand. With complete and accurate information from the debtor, the accountant should be able to quickly formulate a report that can be used to negotiate a fair liquidation or restructuring plan.

If at any time it is determined that the debtor was anything but completely honest, creditors should reevaluate their decision to go along with an out-of-court settlement instead of going through the formal bankruptcy process.

The debtor should keep creditors updated about its financial progress throughout the negotiations. Not doing so would show bad faith on the part of the debtor. Credit professionals should closely monitor these reports to make sure that the financial condition of the creditor is not deteriorating.

Assuming they are not significant, unresolved disputes should be referred to the American Arbitration Association for resolution.

What about the Creditor?

It is not always clear that creditors should agree to out-of-court settlements. Clearly, the lower costs should translate into a larger payout for the unsecured creditors. In evaluating the prospects of a chapter 11 restructuring, creditors are always advised that they should only agree if they will get at least the same amount, if not more, than they would in an outright liquidation. The considerations are no different in an out-of-court settlement.

Some creditors do not like out-of-court settlements because the settlements bind only those who accept it. Thus, some experts recommend that the debtor not accept settlements if only a few are offered.

Summary

As you can see by the amount of space devoted to the topic, bankruptcy can be complicated, yet interesting. We have barely touched the surface. Credit professionals are urged to hire a competent bankruptcy attorney, along with other trained professionals, to help them when a customer files for bankruptcy protection. At the same time, they are urged to learn as much as they can about the topic.

CHAPTER 11

Technology in the Credit and Collections Department

After reading this chapter you will be able to

- Know how technology is being used in credit and collections
- Integrate the use of e-mail into daily operations
- Make the best use of Internet facilities
- Understand and develop your own credit scoring models

Technology has made a massive difference in the way credit and collection functions are handled. Personal computers and use of e-mail are now commonplace in virtually every credit department, and that's just the beginning.

Use in Today's Credit Departments

Technology has been a lifesaver to credit executives who are faced with an ever-growing workload and no additional resources to handle the increased responsibilities. In responding to the most recent *IOMA's Report on Managing Credit Receivables and Collections'* survey, credit professionals shared their success strategies for using technology to improve departmental productivity. Eighteen of the best techniques that were reported were:

1. Develop reports that help staff members maximize their time by prioritizing workflow.

2. Send reminder letters 30 days after the initial invoice via the postal service and e-mail. Credit professionals report that e-mail correspondence is more effective because customers tend to respond quicker. Saving on the cost of postage is an added benefit.

3. Implement new accounts receivable database systems to report on sales and accounts receivable balances efficiently.

4. Automate the cash application process by receiving a computer feed from the lockbox and automatically applying payments. This gets the accounts updated a day earlier and saves half a day of posting.

5. Tighten "payment required with order" stops within a software program. Orders received without a payment are directed to a queue and calls are made for payment.

6. Upgrade computer equipment.

7. Automate invoicing and faxing to the customer.

8. Work with the information technology department to design an automated collection system. Test one area of business, and then tweak and add enhancements as needed before rolling out to the entire company.

9. Use preauthorized debits to collect from any customer that will agree to the process.

10. Integrate new software that distinguishes a customer's credit limit in conjunction with the age of outstanding invoices.

11. Use an optical imaging storage solution to minimize the amount of paper in the credit department.

12. Use invoice storage and retrieval imaging software as an electronic file folder. With the addition of a fax server, the staff can receive credit applications, fax references, pull Dun & Bradstreet reports, and receive credit references without leaving their desks.

13. Update computers and make sure the staff gets adequate training on the new hardware and software acquired.

14. Increase the use of Electronic Data Interchange (EDI) and optical character recognition (OCR) for cash applications.

15. Automate claims resolution with workflow technology.

16. Improve communication with both customers and the sales department by using e-mail.

17. When taking over a group using more than one computer system, say as a result of a merger or acquisition, convert everyone to one system, communicate between brands, and treat all customers uniformly.

18. E-mail, e-mail, e-mail.

Technology is the answer to credit executives' prayers, because it enables departments to do more with less. Review the suggestions that our survey participants made to find one or more that will enable your department to handle the tons of work that comes its way.

Electronic Invoicing

A paperless office has long been the dream of innovative, forward-thinking credit professionals. While it is not yet a reality, certain innovations are bringing this dream closer. Imaging and workflow technology were the first giant steps forward. Lately, there has been another innovation that could bring a paperless office within the reach of virtually every accounts receivable department, and make expensive imaging equipment obsolete in the

E-mail Strategies that Work

- Any communications—including internal with other departments and employees within the credit department and external with customers, service providers, and others in the credit field

- To contact buyers and research customer information

- As a follow up to phone calls, faxes, or mailed copies

- To send and receive credit references

- Multinational companies, finding it difficult to communicate via telephone due to time and language differences are turning to e-mail for help. It is being used to send timely inquiries and responses and also to reduce paper flow

- To send customers copies of requested information such as invoice copies

- To receive all press releases, Form 10K, or Form 10Q for publicly traded customers

- To communicate with customers' accounts payable departments regarding unpaid invoices and unearned cash discounts

- To communicate with sales reps regarding past-due customers

- To request new and updated financial information from customers

- To contact people you cannot get on the phone

- To send reminders and collection letters

- To send notification letters and exchange information with customers

- To reconcile accounts and send spreadsheets by e-mail to customers for that purpose

TIPS & TECHNIQUES CONTINUED

- To share credit information with subsidiary companies
- To communicate with sales reps as well as collections and accounts receivable personnel in remote locations
- To replace any or all types of communications that are sent via mail or fax
- To receive Internet news about both customers and related industries
- To resolve issues that are causing customers not to pay in as quick a fashion as possible
- Instead of calling some large customers, use e-mail to request status of payments, either before they are due or if they are late
- To enlist the help of the sales reps with a problem on an account
- To resolve chargeback issues and properly apply cash
- To handle customer complaints (It is being used with new credit and adjustment systems for online claims to complement existing complaint system)
- To communicate with large customers regarding late payments (There is less room for error if they see the past-due notice rather than copying them down from voice mail. It is also more confidential than faxing)
- To assist with export customer collection problems
- To obtain information on credit and collection topics
- To send invoices to those customers who agree to receive invoices via e-mail
- To send documentation to customers for contracts
- To receive incoming orders from the field and reply where necessary

process. We are talking about electronic invoicing. Representatives from five companies discuss the specifics of the products they offer (no two are identical) and about some of the obstacles billing and accounts receivable professionals run into when they try to implement electronic invoicing.

Electronic invoicing is the delivery of invoices, most likely over the Internet, to a customer's accounts payable department in electronic format. No paper is received—although the invoice can be printed at any time—and the accounts payable department can then forward the invoice, via e-mail, to whoever needs to approve it. The information is then also available, without further keying, to be housed on a network for data retrieval. If it is combined with electronic payments, the information is then forwarded back (without rekeying!) to the vendor.

Why Is Electronic Invoicing Attractive?

In addition to the elimination of mountains of paper, accounts receivable professionals like electronic invoicing because:

- It eliminates mistakes due to rekeyed information.

- There are currently fears about the mail.

- It makes the workflow to route invoices for approval a no-brainer.

- It reduces costs.

- It makes it difficult, if not impossible, for others to blame the mail for their own shortcomings in processing paper.

Usage

So, you ask, if this is such a great deal, why aren't companies signing up en masse? We wondered the same thing and asked the product sponsors. The obstacles include:

- Cost

- Implementation time

- Budget constraints
- Internal resistance to change
- Lack of ease of use
- Difficulty in signing up partners
- Fear

Overcoming the Obstacles

Accounts receivable professionals who can determine why their companies and their customers are holding back are in the best position to offer a counterargument for why electronic invoicing is the right choice.

If budget constraints or cost are issues, iPayables' Kim Rawlings suggests presenting "compelling return-on-investment data to build the business case for the initiative." She is happy to help credit professionals interested in her product make the case. BillingZone recommends the same approach. Its representative points out that EIPP offers both billers and payers a significant value proposition by eliminating paper from the process. It suggests that improved customer service, cash management, and accuracy in tracking and taking discounts are added benefits that can be factored into the equation.

Those facing the anonymous complaints of "it will take too long" or "our customers won't use it" should rely on documentation provided by the service provider. "We lay out a well-defined process and work with clients to ensure that the project is managed," says Open Business Exchange's Martha Perlin. Many of these vague complaints vanish when people understand what is expected of them and how the electronic invoicing process will work.

Fear of the unknown is a concept many accounts receivable professionals have encountered when trying to implement a new process. It is also what many are finding when they mention electronic invoicing in their own shops. "Validating the concept is probably the lengthiest process involved to garner buy-in from companies as a whole," points out Direct Commerce's Lisa Sconyers. "Such an application offers big money savings opportunities as well as extreme process streamlining, but our current economic market has instilled fear and conservatism toward implementing new technology," she concludes.

Sconyers has a few recommendations for credit professionals who find themselves facing this dilemma. She suggests they begin by calling and getting a referral from a customer already using the product. She points out that since her company can quickly and efficiently configure and integrate its application in a matter of days, a pilot program will give potential clients the opportunity to test the product firsthand at no risk.

Selecting the Best Service

A company interested in pursuing the e-invoicing route will base its own decision on its:

- Existing internal processes
- Budget
- Corporate culture
- Willingness to mandate change both internally and externally

Check out the Web sites below for additional information and contact those vendors whose products interest you:

- www.billingzone.com
- www.directcommerce.com
- www.ipayables.com
- www.obexchange.com
- www.xign.com

Although e-invoicing may seem like a leading-edge approach today, in just a few short years it will be commonplace. Remember when the use of P-cards was considered innovative?

Electronic Documents

Electronic documents are the future medium for commerce. Given all the changes in the last few years, the use of electronic documents has taken on new dimensions. Computers communicating with each other now conduct the growth of commerce, not humans using phones or the written word. The exchange of electronic business documents facilitates this.

A standard for these documents that would ease the transition to e-commerce is starting to emerge and is enabling the increasingly sophisticated use of electronic documents. The first such standard was EDI but, as those familiar with it are well aware, it is costly and inflexible. A newer format with emerging standards is becoming the dominant format for e-commerce over the Internet. It is referred to as XML (eXtensible MarkUp Language).

What Is XML?

XML uses documents readable by humans that contain embedded tags for the computers' use as well. XML uses bracket-enclosed tags similar to HTML. With the help of these predefined tags, information can be presented so that both the human and the computer can understand it. Teri Hinder (www.COVANSYS.com) provides a new definition for XML. She calls it the glue that pulls e-commerce together. She claims that all you need to understand about XML is that it is formatted as tag-data-tag.

Here is an example of a well-formed XML document. <greeting type = "friendly">Hello, world!</greeting>. While you may not understand all the formatting that goes along with the sample, you certainly can understand the intent of the message.

Additionally, Hinder says that legal XML documents are called well formed, a well-formed document describes a logical tree, and if a well-formed document conforms to an optional set of constraints (called a DTD) it is also valid.

XML and Standards

One of the most frequent complaints heard about XML is that there is more than one kind of XML. That is only partially true. Currently, there are a few different XMLs but they are all coming together as the different groups continue to work together. Hinder believes that in five years there will be a standard. Accounts payable professionals cannot wait that long to get involved, however.

The emerging leader is something referred to as ebXML (electronic business extensible markup language), which was created in November 1999 as a result of a North Atlantic Treaty Organization meeting. Its charter, says Hinder, was to provide an open XML language-based infrastructure enabling the global use of electronic business information in an interoperable, secure, and consistent manner by all parties in an 18-month period.

Not only did this group meet its goals, but the major players in all current e-commerce initiatives have agreed to follow ebXML as their end state e-commerce standard.

Credit Scoring

Get ready—credit scoring is about to slam the business-to-business (B2B) credit community with the same force that the Internet did just a few years ago. While scoring will not, as many fear, eliminate the credit function, it will radically change the way credit tasks are handled in the e-commerce environment. The Internet is the agent of change forcing this shift. Now, before you turn the page because you believe that your company will not participate in the e-commerce revolution, realize that virtually all companies are investigating B2B e-commerce options. The following sections look at the factors that are affecting the change, and the credit models that are emerging as the likely winners.

Techniques Motivating the Change

Speaking at FCIB's Global Credit Conference, eCredit.com's Kelly Cundiff delineated the three issues that will radically affect the credit transformation at many companies:

1. *The ERP/receivables management disconnect.* In the last few years, many companies have implemented new ERP models, such as SAP, expecting increased functionality across the board. The problem is that many of these models have made life much more difficult for the credit profession by requiring further drill down to get the information that was previously available and taken for granted. "90% of the companies implementing ERP had identified the goal of reducing their DSO," says Cundiff, " but only 30% actually achieved success and that was after an average period of 23 months."

2. *Costly CRM investments create pressure to approve customers.* The move toward e-commerce expensive customer relationship management (CRM) software facilitates the process and puts additional pressure on credit to approve the sale. Cundiff says that some experts believe that the cost of implementing CRMs will be the same as the cost of implementing ERPs cubed! Talk about pressure. Companies spend $650 to lure a repeat buyer. The problem for credit professionals, she says, is that after companies spend large sums of money on these systems, they can't afford to turn away a prospect because of a bad credit decision.

3. *The evolution of online commerce.* In approximately five years, online commerce has evolved from innovative companies having a basic information site to full-fledged e-commerce that supports a full order-to-cash cycle for both new and current business and customers.

Changing Fundamental Assumptions

The preceding factors put tremendous pressure on both the credit and finance functions. Traditionally, taking several hours or days for credit and financing decisions has been acceptable. The reality, says Cundiff, is that today these decisions must be done at Web speed, which is the pressure point for those selling over the Internet. Credit is the last bastion of manual intervention in the order-to-cash cycle, and guess what? It has to change.

In order to avoid the e-business bottlenecks, the credit decision must be made in minutes. If the transaction can't be closed immediately, she warns, there is a 50% chance that the customer will be lost. Most companies are willing to live with odds this high. However, these same institutions will still need high-quality credit decisions.

The order-to-cash cycle is delineated in Exhibit 11.1. Cundiff says the first three steps are the core of the process and must happen at Web speed. Independent studies have shown that these three steps must take five minutes or less to avoid losing the customer. (These same studies show that the customer will be lost if these three steps take longer than 30 seconds!)

While traditionally credit professionals had between four and ten days to get financial reports, gather financial and credit information, analyze the credit, and assign a credit limit or arrange financing, this is no longer feasible. If giving customers a response takes that long, they will go elsewhere. Thus, the credit decision must be at least partially

EXHIBIT 11.1

Order-to-Cash Cycle

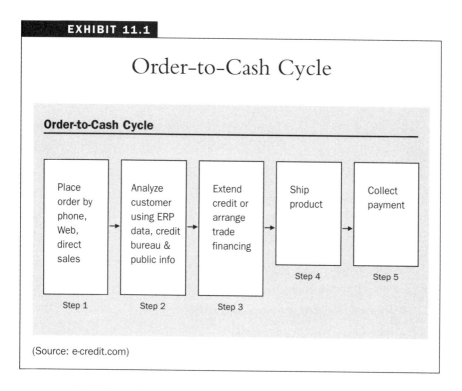

Order-to-Cash Cycle

Place order by phone, Web, direct sales	Analyze customer using ERP data, credit bureau & public info	Extend credit or arrange trade financing	Ship product	Collect payment
Step 1	Step 2	Step 3	Step 4	Step 5

(Source: e-credit.com)

automated. Although many consider the extension of credit to be more of an art than a science, much of it can be automated.

Cundiff says that with the adoption of a credit-scoring model, credit analysts' time can be spent on more top-level tasks, rather than on some of the more tedious credit tasks. The author concurs only partially with this view. The harsh reality is that some lower-level credit jobs will be lost while those positions that remain will be of a higher echelon. We also believe that fighting change is a waste of effort and that credit professionals should learn as much as possible about the new models. With automation, credit analysts focus on the credit value at risk, financial benchmarking and analysis, and active credit management. Information from multiple bureaus can and should be used.

How Decisions Are Automated

In general, credit-scoring models automate the decisions in about 80% of the cases. The remaining 20% fall into that gray area requiring manual intervention and review by an experienced credit professional. Additionally, if a change is made to the credit policy, the professional makes sure the model is changed quickly and thus applied consistently to all future credit decisions. This might occur, for instance, in a slowing economy if a company decided to tighten its credit standards. The same scorecard is used for all customers so subjectivity is removed from the decisions.

Cundiff detailed the requirements for a credit scoring and financing system. They include:

- Full end-to-end process automation
- The ability to access and process data from all credit sources
- Flexible technology for unique scoring rules
- Seamless integration with the accounts receivable system
- The ability to analyze exceptions and large dollar decisions

The integration with the existing accounts receivable system is extremely important. She noted that the best prediction of future payment patterns is past payment history. A company's unique credit policies and rules are stored in the credit model. Then the order can be taken, and the credit decision made while the customer is still in the sales mode.

Worst Practices

Some companies develop what Cundiff calls "work around" solutions for their e-business. She warns that these solutions can create some negative results. Specifically:

- Companies that develop separate online credit policies will find that their customers will figure this out and place their orders accordingly. The company will then have assumed more risk than it intended to.

- Companies that assign automatic credit limits to their online customers could find they are limiting sales when a customer who might qualify for a higher amount limits itself to the limit offered online.

- Some companies refuse to accept new customers over the Internet, which defeats the purpose of e-commerce.

- Some companies take orders over the Internet, but then they delay the credit decision thus risking the loss of that sale (remember the five-minute B2B credit rule).

- Some companies choose to completely automate the credit decision and do not leverage the synergies created by the Internet.

IN THE REAL WORLD

Credit Pro Develops Credit Scoring Model

The story of how one skeptical credit manager developed a credit-scoring model for his company is one all credit pros can learn from. Ron Wells, a credit manager for Chevron in England and the first non-U.S. credit professional to earn the coveted certified credit executive (CCE) designation from the National Association of Credit Managers (NACM), explained how he built the model at the recent FCIB Global Conference in New York. He began by discussing his goals and then gave a detailed breakdown of exactly what he put into the model.

Objectives

Wells says that Chevron wanted to make credit limit decisions in a standardized, systematic, and factual way. Its goal was to make credit decisions that both align with and support the company's overall strategy. It wanted to speed up credit decisions using technology as much as possible. He says that the result of this strategy would be to replace the credit analyst. The credit staff would still be needed, but some of its functions would be eliminated. Wells was a believer that credit analysis is still more of an art than a science so to say that he was a bit dubious would be putting it kindly.

Credit decisions, he says, are typically based on old information, if available, a different set of facts and feelings in each case, and an intuitive weighting system based on personal experience. Those practiced credit professionals reading this will know that what he is saying is true. They also realize that most of the time the traditional way produces a fairly good result. However, the question remains: Is there a better way?

He puts forth the following hypothesis: Is it possible to distill all these factors into a manageable generic list of questions, which require factual answers that can be weighted and thus produce consistent credit decisions? The answer to this question, he was to discover, is *yes*.

Building the Model

The "Sample Credit Scoring Factors with Model Evaluation" section shows the input for the scoring model Wells developed. He says that it is a work in progress because he continues to fine-tune it. If at first glance some of the questions seem a bit odd, Wells has a reason for including them. He says that some of the questions are proxies for other information. He used eCredit.com's CCEx Espert Comments Synthetic Summary Score on the financial information. He judges the customer's financial strength to be:

- Excellent = 100
- Good = 80
- Above average = 60
- Average = 40
- Marginal = 20
- Poor = 0

IN THE REAL WORLD CONTINUED

The scores from the model are then weighted using a simple algebraic formula. Wells did not share his weights, which may change as a company's appetite for risk increases or decreases. The output from the model is a trade credit score.

The credit score is then used in a simple algebraic equation to set a credit limit for the customer. The limit is based on the score and the customer's equity. The better the score, the larger the percent of equity that will be used to determine the allowable credit limit. Wells incorporates the following rules in setting limits:

- The limit shall not exceed 10% of equity amount of own company.

- The limit must not exceed the requested amount, bearing in mind the customer's normal purchasing pattern.

- The limit shall not exceed the customer's assessed ability to pay trade-related obligations in the normal course of business within normal terms. This amount is determined using the credit score and the customer's equity.

For example, a customer with the very highest trade credit rating might be given a line equal to 25% of its shareholder equity, while one with the lowest rating might only be allowed 4% of its shareholder equity. The lowest rating in this case refers to the lowest rating that a company might still be willing to sell on open-account terms.

Before and After

With the system up and running, Wells has a chance to reflect on the benefits of the process. For starters, it should be said, that he appears to have changed his mind and can now see the benefits of credit scoring. Before, he says, each analyst made individual decisions. Now the system drives the decisions, and analysts feed the system. The result of the individual decision making was inconsistent decisions and review of available information. With the system, consistent decisions are made based on a mandatory list of factors.

One of the difficulties with the old approach was that adjusting a firm's appetite for risk is difficult and there was no basis to analyze portfolio risk. With a credit-scoring model, risk appetite can be adjusted by amending the weights or limits in the model. Portfolio risk is apparent, providing risk managers with the information they need to manage that risk.

Using This Information

The model as developed by Wells will not work in every organization. Different companies in different industries with varying appetites for customer payment risk will assess the various factors accordingly. Some will not need to include all the elements used by Wells. For example, a company selling exclusively in the domestic market would not need the country risk component. Others may want to addfactors not included by Wells. However, his work serves as an excellent foundation for those interested in building their own models. Studying his methods and approach will also provide credit professionals with an understanding of credit scoring in the B2B world.

Sample Credit Scoring Factors with Model Evaluations

Following is some information used in Wells' model.

Financial Information

Is audit report clean (unqualified)?

- Yes = 10
- Qualified or unaudited = 0

Is financial information age:

- Less than six months = 10
- Less than one year = 6
- Less than 18 months = 2
- Older = 0

Is amount of equity at risk:

- Greater than twice the proposed limit = 20
- Equal to the proposed limit = 10
- Half the proposed limit = 5
- Less = 0

Is defensive interval:

- Greater than 32 days = 20
- Greater than 16 days = 16
- Greater than eight days = 10
- Greater than four days = 4
- Less = 0

Was operating cash flow minus dividends positive?

- Yes = 20
- No = 0

Is the number of accounts payable days equal to normal payment terms?

- Yes = 20
- Less than 150% of normal = 10
- More = 0

Management Ability and Integrity

Number of years the target company has been in the relevant business:

- More than 15 years = 20
- More than seven years but less than 15 = 10
- Less than seven years = 0

The chief executive officer and chief financial officer are both

- Appointed on merit = 20
- If one or both are family members or political appointees = 0

No scandal in past two years = 10

No dispute with authorities in the past two years = 10

At least one executive was a senior government official or minister or is a political appointee = 10

There is evidence of an effective strategic response to market or competitive forces in the last three years.

- Yes = 30
- No = 0

Alignment with Own Company Strategy

Competitors are offering or providing unsecured credit to customer.

- Yes = 50
- No = 0

Own company wants to increase its market share.

- Yes = 20
- No = 0

Potential margin is:

- High = 50
- Medium = 20
- Low = 5

Potential outlet for otherwise "no value goods" or "high retention cost goods"?

- Yes = 40
- No = 0

Transactions would support strategies of a fellow operating unit.

- Yes = 20
- No = 0

Transactions could lead to acquisition of additional business.

- Yes = 20
- No = 0

IN THE REAL WORLD CONTINUED

Country Risk

Headquartered in an Organization for Economic Cooperation and Development member country?

- Yes = 100 (see other questions)
- No = 0

Thompson Bank Watch Country Rating is:

- AAA/AA = 40
- A/BBB = 30
- BB = 20
- CCC = 10
- CC = 5
- C/D = 0

Your politically sensitive or essential goods as a percentage of domestic consumption are:

- More than 75% = 40
- More than 50% = 30
- More than 25% = 20
- Less = 0

Headquartered in a country strategically important to your company?

- Yes = 20
- No = 5

E-commerce and the need for quick credit decisions is making the use of credit scoring mandatory for many companies. Credit professionals who want to survive and thrive in the next decade will need to learn everything about these models and how to use them. Are you ready?

Digital Signatures and Encryption

Two new technologies that will ease your boss's fears about Internet security are coming to credit and collections—quickly. They are encryption and digital signatures. James M. Burstedt, Chevron's manager of reengineering, and Ed Ames, a Chevron analyst for e-commerce, explained these approaches at several conferences, and explained how their company's policies are changing because of them.

Chevron's Corporate Policy

Chevron's policy allows it to protect its most important asset, its information, from hackers, pranksters, dishonest insiders, competitors, and information terrorists. It is concerned about viruses, interception, prying eyes, alteration or loss of data, communication blocks, and system disruptions. Its biggest concern, however, is unauthorized access. The policy states,

> Information and the systems supporting it are key company assets, requiring prudent and proactive protection by information owners and users alike. It is the policy of the company to secure these assets from external and internal threats through a combination of technology, practices, processes and monitoring, based on risk and the value of the assets. The goal is to minimize the potential for damage, either purposeful or accidental, to the company's computer and communications systems, company data, and information.

Origins of the Problem and Its Solutions

The speakers pointed out that security breaches could arise from:

- An intruder masquerading as an employee
- Eavesdropping
- Data being changed en route

- E-mail addresses being changed en route
- Cracked passwords and identifications (IDs)

The speakers also identified the defenses that stop unauthorized access to computer information transferred over the Internet, including:

- Authentication (digital signature–private key/hash)
- Encryption
- Digital certificates (ID validation/nonrepudiation)
- Firewalls
- Strong passwords

The consequences of not having these defenses can be severe. Financial loss, damage to the company's reputation, loss of business, legal actions, and the loss of strategic information are only a few of the results.

When an employee has a laptop stolen, the biggest loss is not the cost of the laptop, but the strategic information stored on the hard drive. Thus, Chevron relies on what it calls "secured messaging."

Secured Messaging

Chevron defines secured messaging as the use of encryption and digital signatures. A digital signature is *not* a digitized signature—an individual's manual signature on an electronic device such as those certain department stores use for charge card purchases. Burstedt and Ames provided the following definitions:

- *Digital signature.* Digital signatures are unique for a person and use a private key to verify something as belonging specifically to and used solely by that person. It is linked to data, so any change to the data will invalidate the signature. It is also nonreputable, which means that a person can prove he or she sent a communication and, conversely, cannot deny that he or she sent it. It is the equivalent in the paper world to getting a document notarized.

- *Encryption.* This is the ability to transform electronic information into an unreadable format that only authorized individuals can convert back to its original readable format.

- *Encryption engines.* Also known as encryption algorithms, they are now powerful enough to generate truly random keys, taking this responsibility off people's hands. They also allow session keys to be used once or multiple times and then discarded.

Back to Math Class

Upon reading the word *algorithm*, some credit and collection professionals may vaguely remember high-school math class. An algorithm is a detailed sequence of calculations performed during a specific number of steps to achieve a desired outcome.

A *hash algorithm* is a function that reduces a message to a mathematical expression that cannot be reversed (*one-way hash*). For example, if every letter of the alphabet were assigned a number (a = 1, b = 2, and so on), any name could be reduced to a single digit. The speakers chose Julius Caesar because he was one of the earliest users of encryption.

J	U	L	I	U	S		C	A	E	S	A	R
10	21	12	9	21	19		3	1	5	19	1	18

The sum for Julius = 92   The sum for Caesar = 47

$9 + 2 = 11$ $4 + 7 = 11$

$11 + 11 = 22$

$2 + 2 = 4$

Therefore, the hash total for Julius Caesar is 4.

Altering any original message or file, including changing the spelling of a word, eliminating apostrophes, or changing a comma to a period, will result in a different hash.

PKI

Messages are encrypted and decrypted using public and private keys. As commerce continues to move to the Internet, expect to hear much more about public key infrastructure (PKI). The speakers also offered a clear explanation of how these keys are used. "Two sets of electronic keys are used to encrypt and decrypt documents. Public keys can be shared, while only their specific owner knows private keys. An encrypted document is created using the sender's private key and the receiver's public key. The receiver decrypts the document using the sender's public key and the receiver's private key. The public key is the certificate authority. Separate pairs of keys can be used to encrypt or digitally sign to strengthen security.

"Whatever is locked by a private key can only be unlocked by the corresponding public key and vice versa. Encrypting and sending with the sender's private key and the receiver's public key can therefore only be decrypted with the receiver's private key and the sender's public key. Use the private key to create the digital signature/hash."

Currently, a huge debate is going on over setting standards for the PKI that will not be settled soon, because a number of entities have a vested interest in becoming the standard setter. These concepts may be new to many reading this, but we believe that for anyone who works for a company that uses the Internet, understanding these concepts is imperative. Remember, not too long ago the whole idea of the Internet seemed alien.

Summary

As you can see, technology is radically changing the way the credit, collection, and accounts receivable function is handled. This is just the beginning. Follow these and any new developments closely—your job could depend on it.

CHAPTER 12

Professionalism and the Future of the Credit Profession

After reading this chapter you will be able to

- Understand what will be required to be a credit professional in the twenty-first century
- Identify the educational opportunities available to keep your skills up-to-date
- Find the necessary resources to keep your skills top-notch
- Evaluate the certification opportunities

The credit profession is an ever-evolving one. Those who are successful tend to be those who realize that professional education never ends. That's right—you're never finished with school. Those that get ahead not only work hard and keep up-to-date on credit and all the fields that affect credit, they also continually network.

Industry Groups

There's no one who knows your customers better than your competition. Now normally, businesspeople don't discuss their customers with the competition. However, in the credit profession this is not true. Industry credit groups are typically run by credit associations. They provide a collective intelligence on customer payment habits and financial status, giving their members an edge in identifying credit risks and solving collection problems.

At group meetings, members are very careful to talk only about the past not future plans. Typically, they are run by an association member who keeps notes. The groups are very careful not to collude or have any conversations that might be misconstrued as restraint of trade. The information shared at these meetings is for use in the credit departments only and is not shared with sales.

Credit Associations

There are numerous professional associations for credit professionals. They include:

- *National Association of Credit Management.* In June 1896, 82 delegates from several local credit groups met in Toledo, Ohio, to endorse a national movement for the exchange of credit information. Their exchange of credit information was at first conducted on a local and regional level. The association expanded into the National Association of Credit Management (NACM), which today with its network of Affiliated Associations, represents 30,000 credit executives worldwide, making NACM one of the oldest and largest business organizations in the United States. The NACM members are served by 52 Affiliated Associations throughout the country and by NACM-National, the national headquarters office. An annual conference, a certification program, education, and much more are some of the benefits offered by the NACM. Additional information about this extensive group can be found on its Web site at www.nacm.org.

- *Credit Research Foundation.* The Credit Research Foundation (CRF) is a nonprofit, member-supported, education, and

Surviving and Succeeding in a Twenty-First Century Credit Department

- Earn at least a BA or BS. If you don't have one, go back to school. Prospective employers often use the degree to determine who they will interview—and who they won't.

- Keep your credit skills up-to-date. This means following the latest changes in laws affecting credit, learning how to use the latest technology, and much, much more.

- Consider studying for some of the NACM's accreditations.

- Consider going back to school for an MBA.

- Learn as much accounting as you can.

- Network with your peers.

- Manage your relationship with your boss and anyone in the organization likely to become your boss at some time in the future.

- Polish your writing and public speaking skills.

- Get as much exposure outside your company as possible—but don't brag about it internally. The exposure outside is necessary should your company be forced to lay you off. Bragging about it internally may cause a jealous reaction.

- Whenever possible, do favors for others. You'll be surprised how often you get paid back in ways you never expected.

- Make sure your computer skills are top notch.

- Learn a little about international credit even if your company has no international activity—now.

- If possible, take on responsibilities in other areas thus potentially making yourself a reasonable candidate for higher-level jobs.

research organization dedicated to the credit and financial management community. It conducts surveys, most notably its quarterly days sales outstanding (DSO) survey, research, and three meetings a year. For additional information, visit its Web site at www.crfonline.org.

- *Riemer Group.* The Riemer organization runs industry credit groups, collects trade data, and runs an annual conference. Its members are loyal and speak highly of its services. Additional information can be found at www.riemer.com.

- *National Group Management Corp.* This group runs numerous industry credit groups. It is headquartered in Philadelphia and can be reached at (215) 923-1765.

- *Media Credit Association.* This group is a division of the Magazine Publishers Association. It holds several educational meetings a year. Additional information can be found at www.magazine.org.

- *Vendor Compliance Group.* This is a relatively new group that focuses on vendor compliance. Information can be found at www.vca.org.

Certifications

The NACM sponsors three professional designations that enable credit professionals to demonstrate their commitment to excellence in their field. The NACM is the only body that offers these nationally recognized, professional designations. These certifications include:

- *The Credit Business Associate (CBA)* is an academic-based designation that signals mastery of three business credit-related disciplines:

    1. Introductory financial accounting

2. Business credit principles

3. Introductory financial statement analysis

There is no minimum work experience requirement for this designation level and the course work needed to qualify can be obtained through colleges, local NACM Affiliated Association programs, self-study, or nationally sponsored programs. The CBA Designation Exam is administered three times a year at local NACM Affiliated Associations and at the NACM annual convention.

- *The Credit Business Fellow (CBF)* is an academic- and participation-based designation that illustrates that achievers are knowledgeable about and have contributed to the field of business credit by first having earned the CBA designation as well as having completed additional course work. The CBF designation signals competence in:

  - Introductory finance

  - Intermediate financial statement analysis

  - Basic principles of management

  - Business and credit law

  Credit Business Fellow designation applicants must have accumulated 75 NACM Career Roadmap points and pass the CBF Designation Exam. The CBF designation exam is administered three times a year at local NACM Affiliated Associations and at the NACM annual convention.

- The *Certified Credit Executive (CCE)* is NACM's highest designation, which endorses its achievers as capable of managing the credit function at an executive level. Candidates must have a minimum of ten years experience plus a four-year degree, or have earned the CBA and CBF designations and have 125 NACM Career Roadmap points. Candidates must pass the rigorous, four-hour CCE Designation Exam, which tests application skills in the areas of:

- Accounting
- Finance
- Domestic and international credit concepts
- Management and law

Certified credit executives are required to recertify every three years until reaching 60 years of age, further endorsing their commitment to continuing education, self-improvement, and advancement of the business credit profession.

International

As the economy becomes more global at an ever-increasing speed, those who wish to succeed and get ahead in their careers will be forced to learn more about the trappings of the international arena. Credit and collection procedures in other countries are quite different than they are in the United States. Credit insurance is used more frequently, as are things like forfeiting, avals, and many other processes that initially will seem alien to those used to the way credit and collections are handled domestically. Additionally, the issue of cultural differences opens a door on different behavior, customer relations and, frankly, expectations.

The credit manager who does not expect customers in other countries to behave and react differently is in for a big surprise and possibly big losses. When first presented with an international account, many domestic credit professionals either do nothing or treat the customer as a domestic account. This can result in either selling to a customer who does not meet credit standards, or offending a perfectly good customer and ultimately losing that account.

Those who want successful long-term careers in credit need to add international skills to their arsenal of weapons. It isn't too difficult, and it is quite interesting. The educational opportunities are numerous.

There are a number of organizations devoted to providing information to international credit executives. Some make it their entire focus while others include international topics as part of their educational efforts. These groups include:

- *FCIB.* The best known of the international credit groups is the FCIB, a branch of the NACM. The entire focus of this group is international. The FCIB has four luncheon roundtable meetings each year in New York. These meetings may include an educational speaker. However, the focal point to the gatherings is the country-by-country reviews by the attendees. Information is submitted prior to the meeting and summarized by the FCIB staff. Attendees offer their views and experiences in the given countries.

  The FCIB also runs several annual conferences in the United States and three abroad. These educational events run for a day and a half and feature experts on topics of interest to the members. Roundtable discussions are typically part of the gatherings, as well.

  The FCIB has also introduced a professional certification, the CICE. Information about this program and other FCIB information can be obtained at www.fcibglobal.com.

- *Riemer.* The well-known and highly respected Riemer Group is best known for its many industry credit trade groups. One of the groups is an international group. Meetings are held several times a year to discuss trade experiences. An educational speaker is usually part of the meetings.

Each fall, as part of its annual conference, the Riemers bring in a number of educational speakers who focus on international matters. Typically, the conference occurs in early September and the first two days are devoted to international topics. For more information about Riemer activities and services, go to www.riemer.com.

- *Unz Co.* Originally a publisher of export related forms, Unz has expanded its focus to include educational activities as they relate to international trade. The company offers a number of seminars on topics such as Incoterms, letters of credit, and the like. For more information, go to www.unzcompany.com.

- *ICM.* The ICM is the professional credit association for the United Kingdom. Each year it offers over 100 day and two-day seminars. Anyone visiting the United Kingdom is advised to check out its Web site to see the extensive schedule to see if they can fit one of these seminars into their schedule. For additional information, go to www.icm.org.uk.

- *Advanstar.* Each year in London, Advanstar runs what it bills as the credit event of the year. Typically held in the spring, this one and a half day event features both seminars and an exhibit hall.

Publishing Resources

There are several credit newsletters and numerous books. The best (okay I'm biased) of these are:

- *IOMA's Report on Managing Credit Receivables and Collections* (newsletter)

- *International Credit and Collections: A Guide to Extending Credit Worldwide.* Mary S. Schaeffer. New York: John Wiley & Sons, Inc., 2001.

The Internet

There are several free credit newsletters available through the Internet. These are of varying quality and can be obtained by accessing the following Web sites:

- www.creditman.co.uk
- www.creditworthy.com
- www.gsc.com

Getting Ahead: Managing Your Boss

Why do some credit executives seem to get ahead much more quickly than others? The answer is not complicated. Successful managers realize that it is not enough to simply perform above expectations. Doing a great job is only half the battle. These respected managers also carefully manage the relationship with their bosses, recognizing that they will never get anywhere if their bosses do not like them, suspect them of being disloyal, or do not respect them. They actively manage the relationships with their superiors. Here's how they do it:

- *Walk a mile in his shoes.* Understand that your boss's priorities may be very different from your own. Take the time to reflect on the problems that your boss faces. Then frame your requests and plan your actions in a manner that will help resolve your boss's problems. If you are aware that your boss is constantly in conflict with the chief financial officer (CFO), don't ask him or her to take an unpopular proposal to the CFO. Rather, recommend a change in procedures that the CFO is likely to agree with. By putting your boss in a position where he or she can look good, you will have taken the first step to building a better relationship.

There will be times when it is necessary to ask for approval for an unpopular proposal. However, if you lay the groundwork by recommending actions that are in line with the CFO's way of thinking, you will be a little closer to getting the approval you need. By keeping any problems your boss may be encountering with his or her boss in the back of your mind, you may be able to position your unpopular request in a way as that makes it more palatable to those reviewing it.

- *Communications.* Good communications is key to building a productive relationship with your boss. This means relaying not only the good news but also the bad. Negative reports about you, your department, or one of your staffers should come from you rather than someone else. By relaying the news yourself, you minimize its impact. This also gives you the opportunity to couch the news in the best possible terms. It also allows you to explain any extenuating circumstances before your boss sees red.

   Notifying your boss of any problems puts him or her in the best position to respond when someone higher in the chain raises the problem. If the company's key customer is upset and is threatening to call the company president, let your boss know in time to prepare for it. By providing the facts, you will help him or her respond intelligently when the inevitable call comes from the president.

   Another benefit to good lines of communication is that you will know what your boss's priorities are. This will help you when making proposals.

- *Manage upward.* Successful credit and collection managers realize that not only do they have to manage their staff, they also have to manage the relationship with their bosses. They

IN THE REAL WORLD

The Dream Job

Leessa Black has a job most credit professionals would give their eyeteeth to have. When she was hired as the first credit manager of Whitewood Industries, she had the opportunity to set up the credit department from scratch, her way, with the CFO's backing. Before she was hired, she said the company had no formal credit policy. The company had a part-time collector and that was the extent of the credit and collection focus. When a customer placed its first order, it was required to pay cash-in-advance for half the order. If the customer paid the remainder on time, it was given open-account terms. Black says that very little information was gathered and customers were not asked to provide tax identification (ID) numbers.

When she started, she pulled each customer account file and updated it with current financials, a credit application and tax ID forms. To establish the company's name in the industry and in order to receive customer payment information, she joined several professional organizations including Reimer, Lyons Mercantile Credit Association, the NACM, and the Furniture Manufacturers' Credit Association.

She wrote a credit and collections manual for credit management, the sales force, and the customer service department. This alerted everyone to what the new ground rules were. She also created a new legal credit application, a form to use to obtain tax ID numbers, and reports for management. She developed an aged trial balance report, DSO reports, monthly statements on all past-due accounts, and a report about calls made on past-due accounts.

She still has occasional disagreements with sales, but says that slowly as she works on keeping the lines of communication open, they come around to seeing things her way. She says that it is extremely important that credit professionals communicate to sales that credit is there to enhance sales not detract from them. Although Black has accomplished a lot, she still has big plans for additional improvements she would like to make as the company continues to grow.

begin this by proving they are loyal. Building trust is crucial to any good alliance and usually takes time. If your boss perceives that you are not loyal to him or her, it will be virtually impossible to build a good relationship. Thus, it is imperative that any time you do something that would show such loyalty, you relate the incident to your boss. You will want to find a way to work it into a conversation without sounding too obsequious.

One of the ways that credit managers show their loyalty is practicing discretion in their conversations. Problems in the department should be kept within the group—especially if the problem is likely to embarrass your boss with his peers. The same goes for any mistakes your boss may make.

Once you have proven your loyalty, you will be in a position to disagree should a difference of opinion arise. Such clashes should take place in private. If you choose to initiate such discussions in public, you inevitably will lose the battle and find yourself uninvited to future events where you would have the opportunity to showcase your talents. Not only will you suffer, the whole department will suffer as well.

Yes, it takes time to build a good relationship, but the time invested in such an endeavor will pay off both for you and your staff. Credit managers who invest the time to manage their relationships with their superiors will find their upward mobility increasing.

Summary

What was the last course or credit seminar you attended? When was the last time you updated your technology or accounting skills? Have you been networking with your peers?

Index

A

Accounts (*see* customers)
Accounts payable, 134
Accounts payable turnover, 9
Accounts receivable issues, 81–101
Accounts receivable aging, 93
ACH (*see* automated clearinghouse)
ACH debit programs, 96–97
ADR (*see* alternative dispute resolution)
Advanstar, 248
Algorithm, hash, 238
Alternative dispute resolution (ADR), 180–182
   arbitration, 180–182
   mediation, 180
American Arbitration Association (AAA), 180, 182
Anderson, Karen, 177–178
Antecedent debt, 209–211
Arbitration (*see* alternative dispute resolution)
Association for Financial Professionals, 95
Automated clearinghouse (ACH), 94–97
Automatic stay, 188

B

Bad-debt reserves, 87, 89–90
Bad-debt write-offs, 91–92, 94
Balance sheet, 8
Balance sheet test, 185
Bankruptcy, 183–214
   filings, 10
   leases and, 187–188
   payouts, order of, 199–200
   reclamation, 200–202

   proof of claim, 189, 200, 202–205
   small claims in, 205–206
Billing:
   best practices 35–36
   electronic (*see* electronic billing)
BillingZone, 40, 46
Black, Leessa, 251
Blakeley, Scott, 171, 186, 199
Business credit, 1
Bust-outs 169–170

C

Carmenni, Al, 24
Cash:
   burn rate, 11
   collateral, 190
   discounts, 97
Cash-in-advance (CIA), 31
Cash-on-delivery (COD), 31
CBA (*see* credit business associate)
CBF (*see* credit business fellow)
CCE (*see* certified credit executive)
Certified credit executive (CCE), 208, 245
Certified expert witness program, 208
Chapter 7, 184, 191–99
Chapter 11, 184, 186
Chapter 11 plan, 190
Chapter 12, 184
Chapter 13, 184
CIA (*see* cash-in-advance)
Claims process, 189
Clayton Act, 166
COD (*see* cash-on-delivery)
Collection(s), 49–79
   agencies, 71–74
   effectiveness index, 86

e-mail use, tips, strategies, 59,
218–219
fax machine use and tips, 55, 57–58
general advice and tips, 50–53
letter guidelines and tips, 53–57
notes, 73
other approaches, 69–71
sales group and, 63–64, 127
telephone guidelines and tips, 60–63
Contemporaneous exchange (*see*
preference action defenses)
Cram-downs, 207–208
Credit:
approval, creative approach, 14
documents, 22
file, 21–24
five Cs of, 12
groups (*see* industry groups)
international (*see* international
credit)
limits, 25
reports, 4, 25–26
scoring, 224–236
role of, 118
software, 26–27
Credit business associate (CBA), 244
Credit business fellow (CBF), 245
Credit Research Foundation (CRF),
64, 97, 242
Creditors:
committee, 189, 206–207
meeting of, 188
Creim, Bill, 22, 24, 158
CRF (*see* Credit Research
Foundation)
Cundiff, Kelly, 225–228
Customer disclosure forms, 170–171
Customer visits, 133–138, 143–146
Customers:
existing, 16–20
new, 14–16, 23
reviewing for large exposures, 20
Cutoff date, 99–100

D

D&B (*see* Dun & Bradstreet)
Days Sales Outstanding (DSO), 9,
85–87, 99
Debt to tangible net worth, 10
Debtor-in-possession, 186
Deduction management:
companies, 105
software, 105
Digital signatures, 236–237
Direct Commerce, 41, 45–46
Discounts:
for early payment, 3
unearned, 4, 100, 103–104
DSO (*see* Days Sales Outstanding)
Dun and Bradstreet (D&B), 4, 17

E

eCredit.com, 225
EDI (*see* Electronic Data Interchange)
EIPP (*see* Electronic Invoice
Presentment and Payment)
Electronic:
billing, 36–48
documents, 223–224
invoicing, 217–223
Electronic Data Interchange (EDI), 217
Electronic Invoice Presentment and
Payment (EIPP), 40
Encryption, 236–238
Encryption engines, 238
Equal Credit Opportunity Act, 166
Equity test, 185
Escheat, 176–179

F

FCIB, 225, 247
Fennelly, Jane, 158
Financial statements, 6–9
age, 7
audited, 6
compiled, 6
documents included in, 7–9
reviewed, 6

Footnotes, 8, 10
Fraud, 168–169

G

GAAP (generally accepted accounting principles) 6
Gross profit margin, 10
Guaranty:
  personal, 148
  of collection, 149

H

Hinder, Terri, 223–224

I

ICM, 248
Income statement, 7
Industry groups, 241
International credit, 26
International trips, 138–142
  researching cultural differences, 142–143
Inventory turnover, 10
Invoice(s), 29–34
  due date, 32
  information included on, 33
  electronic (*see* electronic invoicing)
  timing, 30
IOMA, xv
IPayables, 40, 47–48

J

Joint checks, 149

L

Late fees, 64–68
Leases (*see* bankruptcy)
Letter(s) of credit, 147–156
  back-to-back, 153
  compliance problems, 155
  deferred payment, 151–152
  discrepancy problems, 155
  history of, 153
  reviewing, 154
  revolving, 151
  standby, 151, 156
  timing problems, 154
  transferable, 152

M

Magazine Publishers of America (MPA), 35
Margolin, Weiner & Evans (MW& E), 170
Mechanics liens, 149
Media Credit Association, 35, 244
Mediation (*see* alternative dispute resolution)
Miller Act, 166
Monnat, Mike, 181
MPA (*see* Magazine Publishers of America)

N

NACM (National Association of Credit Management), 163, 208, 242
National Group Management Corp., 244
New value (*see* preference action defenses)

O

OCR (*see* optical character recognition)
Open account, 3
Open Business Exchange, 41, 43–44
Optical character recognition (OCR), 217
Order-to-cash cycle, 226–227
Ordinary course of business (*see* preference action defenses)
Out-of-court settlements, 212

P

Paychex, 181
Payment history, 12
Payment terms, 4, 30–32
Payouts (*see* bankruptcy)

PKI (*see* public key infrastructure)
PMSI (*see* purchase money security
   interest)
Preferences, 196
Preference action defenses, 211–212
Preferential transfer, 209–210
Profit margin(s), 2, 12
Proof of claim (*see* bankruptcy)
Proxicom, 75
Public key infrastructure (PKI), 239
Purchase money security interest
   (PMSI), 158
Purchase orders, 83–85

Q
Quick ratio, 9

R
Ratio analysis, 9–10
Reclamation (*see* bankruptcy)
References, 5
Reorganization plan (*see* chapter 11
   plan)
Retailers, 105–106
Riemer Group, 244, 247
Robinson-Patman Act, 66, 164–165,
   167–168

S
Sales (group), 13, 115
   and non-creditworthy customers,
      127–130
   collections and, 63–64, 127
   educating about credit, 125–126
   meetings, 123
   tips for helping, 124–125
Sales-credit encounters, 116–117
Sales-credit relationship, 116, 118–123
Secured messaging, 237
Security agreement, 158
Security interest, 148, 157–162
SIC codes (*see* Standard Industry
   Classification codes)
Small claims (*see* bankruptcy)

Small claims court, 92
Software (*see* credit)
Standard Industry Classification (SIC)
   codes 10
Statements (*see* financial statements)
Statement of cash flow, 8

T
Technology in credit and collections,
   215–240
Terms (*see* payment terms)
Trade references (*see* references)
Treasury Management Association
   (*see* Association for Financial
   Professionals)
Trustees, 194–195

U
UCC (*see* Uniform Commercial Code)
UCC-1 statements, 147, 158–161
Unauthorized deductions, 104–114
Unclaimed property (*see* escheat)
Unclaimed Property Recovery &
   Reporting Inc. (UPRR),
   177–178
Unearned discount (*see* discounts)
Unz Co., 248
USWest, 37–39

V
Vendor Compliance Group, 244

W
Warning signs, 25
Wells, Ron, 229

X
Xign, 42–43
XML, 223–224